you can
FLOURISH

A Wellness Workbook to Help
You Thrive and Feel Your Best

CHERYL RICKMAN

YOU CAN FLOURISH

Copyright © Cheryl Rickman, 2023

An Hachette UK Company
www.hachette.co.uk

Vie Books, an imprint of Summersdale Publishers Ltd
Part of Octopus Publishing Group Limited
Carmelite House
50 Victoria Embankment
LONDON
EC4Y 0DZ
UK

www.summersdale.com

Printed and bound in Poland

ISBN: 978-1-80007-681-5

Substantial discounts on bulk quantities of Summersdale books are available to corporations, professional associations and other organizations. For details contact general enquiries: telephone: +44 (0) 1243 771107 or email: enquiries@summersdale.com.

Disclaimer
The author and the publisher cannot accept responsibility for any misuse or misunderstanding of any information contained herein, or any loss, damage or injury, be it health, financial or otherwise, suffered by any individual or group acting upon or relying on information contained herein. None of the views or suggestions in this book is intended to replace medical opinion from a doctor who is familiar with your particular circumstances. If you have concerns about your health, please seek professional advice.

CONTENTS

INTRODUCTION:
FLOURISHING AND
FEELING IT ALL

Let me be something every minute
of every hour of my life.

Francie Nolan in *A Tree Grows in*
***Brooklyn* by Betty Smith**

I *love* this life-affirming declaration by dear Francie Nolan, because *being* something and *feeling* something in "every blessed minute" is what, for me, flourishing is all about, whether that is, as Frankie says, "happy or sad, cold or warm".

She goes on to say, "Let me be gay; let me be sad. Let me be hungry... have too much to eat," before saying she wants to be "ragged or well dressed", "sincere" or "deceitful", "truthful" or "a liar". Frankie wants to "be something every blessed minute. And dream all the time so not one little piece of living is ever lost." And this is how we experience life in all its beautiful yet brutal glory, across the entire spectrum of human emotion and lived experience. Feelings of sorrow, disappointment, envy and regret are a normal, integral and even valuable part of what it means to be human. Despite what we've been conditioned to believe about happiness as the holy grail of life, feeling *better* isn't always about feeling *good*.

Feeling better, as we'll explore across these pages, is about *feeling* it all – becoming better at being sad, happy and everything in between, in order to cope with the tough stuff and hope for the good. It's about experiencing the best and worst of life, and still being able to function; to sometimes find the calm equilibrium in between and be gentle with ourselves as we navigate the ups and downs of this roller coaster called life. We need to get to know what makes us think and feel the way we do, and learn to optimize the healthy and minimize the unhealthy. Because how we think and how we feel influences what we do and how we live.

Flourishing = optimal human functioning

Yes, flourishing means more than simply *feeling* good – it's about fulfillment, connection and growth. It's about how we experience life and how well we operate. It's about developing the capacity to build and optimize our well-being in a way that gives our lives meaning. Conversely, languishing, or suffering, is about functioning poorly, staying stuck in an unpleasant, unhealthy and unfulfilled way of living, where well-being diminishes.

Thankfully it is possible to lift ourselves out of this state to be able to flourish. *You Can Flourish* aims to equip you with tools that enable flourishing, by providing a solid toolkit to help you fret less and flourish more – but in a way that gives you permission to be human, mess up, feel bad sometimes and navigate a way forward through (not around) the rough and the smooth, the ups and the downs, the twists and the turns. It's a guide that says if a heart aches, let it ache. It's a guide to navigating the inevitable roller coaster ride of life as best you can, in a way that best serves you and honours your capacity to feel what you need to and flourish.

Positive psychology

Twenty years ago, a new field of psychology called "positive psychology" emerged, defined as "the scientific study of optimal human functioning with the central aim of discovering and promoting the factors that cause individuals and communities to thrive". I first wrote about flourishing in 2013, when I was living in a quaint Hampshire village in southern England with my then four-year-old daughter. I now have a teenager while I go through menopause – a hormonal dance that creates a double dose of big feelings. Much else has changed in my life – and all our lives – since then. I'm looking at *you*, pandemic!

Since writing my self-help debut over a decade ago, I am now a positive psychology practitioner. My family and I left our village and moved to more rural countryside and I've written a whole bookshelf of books about loneliness, happiness, resilience and "enoughness". Changes abound in the world of psychology and wellness too. In addition to a global pandemic, we are now living through a mental health epidemic, with cases of depression and anxiety rising. Furthermore, there have been developments in the field of neuroscience in relation to "interoception" – the way we feel and recognize our emotions through our body – and the concepts of hopefulness.

Up until American psychologists Martin Seligman, Ray Fowler and Mihaly Csikszentmihalyi "invented" the new field of positive psychology in 1998, traditional psychology focused only on undoing what was seen as wrong: removing depression, anxiety or psychosis and getting those suffering mentally back to neutral. However, Seligman and his team realized that mental health isn't just the absence of mental illness, just as happiness isn't just the absence of sadness and good isn't just the absence of bad. Indeed, after devoting 35 years of his life to "undoing depression and helplessness", Seligman and his fellow positive psychology pioneers realized that "the absence of ill-being does not equal the presence of well-being", because "not getting it wrong does not equal getting it right". Having treated patients for 15 years, Seligman found that by the end of treatment, people's misery had been neutralized and they were back to "zero". But, he says, "Did I get a happy patient? No, I got an empty patient. Because the skills for cultivating positive emotion, engagement, meaning, and good relationships differ entirely from those used to fight anger, anxiety and depression."

Positive psychology was born from the question, what if increasing well-being is not just about decreasing ill-being? And what if, rather than just focusing on mental illness and getting mentally unwell people back to neutral, we also focus on mental *wellness* – on getting people *north of neutral*? So that's what Seligman and a team of experts explored over the following decades. More recently, a second wave of positive psychology (positive psychology 2.0) has emerged in response to the culture of enforced positivity, effortless perfection and blind optimism that can pressure us into being happy, victorious and glorious. This evolution, while still focusing on building and sustaining well-being, recognizes and honours the polarity and importance of the interplay between positive and negative.

Positive psychology 2.0 builds on the science of optimal functioning and what constitutes a life well-lived, to incorporate other inevitable parts of the human experience that are as useful and worthy as gratitude, altruism and character – such as sorrow, longing and regret. It honours the idea that both sadness and gladness are bridges to flourishing. It balances realistic optimism and hope with an acceptance of the inevitability of suffering and offers ways to cope. *You Can Flourish* unmasks the benefits of negative emotion, so we can normalize and express all our feelings and boost our well-being.

However, because human beings have an inbuilt negativity bias – which means we are wired to pay more attention to negative and possibly threatening stimuli (see page 19) – this book also recognizes the importance of countering the (often inaccurate) negative stories we tell ourselves by questioning and reframing them, and by building positive emotions and other branches of well-being that enable flourishing. Because flourishing is a more plausible and attainable aim than happiness.

From happiness to flourishing

When parents are asked what they want most for their children, the answer is usually that they are healthy and happy. These are the priorities. However, the psychologists, scientists and researchers behind positive psychology knew that happiness, like other emotions, is merely a fleeting feeling. It doesn't last.

Flourishing, on the other hand, is a way of being, a way of growing and thriving, which is more sustainable and, crucially, more measurable. The psychologists delved into all areas that could enable flourishing. They brought in experts on good character traits, hope theories and areas of sociology, such as interpersonal interaction and human agency. These areas of scientific research focused not just on efficacy studies – which had been the norm until then, using a control group/placebo to carry out research – but *effectiveness* studies, where real-world usage of therapies and interventions was meticulously examined. They analyzed data to prove the degree to which these interventions impact how we function. Subsequently, they came up with five measurable elements – the pillars that comprise optimal well-being, the foundations and formula for human flourishing. They gave this "human dashboard" the mnemonic PERMA.

- **Positive emotion.** Feelings of joy, awe, gratitude, love, interest, serenity, hope, inspiration, pride, amusement.
- **Engagement.** Using skills and competencies to achieve a sense of "flow" and absorption in an activity.
- **Relationships.** Supportive, meaningful, life-enhancing social relationships.
- **Meaning.** Finding fulfillment, purpose and meaning in our experiences.

- **Accomplishment.** Growth and personal development that comes from inspired action and achieving goals.

If we can tick these boxes, each creates a virtuous circle feeding the next; therefore the more engagement and meaning our life has the more likely we are to accomplish our goals. This creates positive emotion, which enhances our ability to build positive relationships, engage in our work and so forth. The stronger our support network, the more likely we are to experience positive emotion and achieve.

But there's one more "pillar of well-being" to add to this list. While studying the mind–body connection, student of Professor Seligman, Emiliya Zhivotovskaya – who founded the Flourishing Center in New York and happened to train me in positive psychology – expanded the original definition by adding:

- **Vitality.** Optimal wellness; strong, healthy bodies.

...thus creating the PERMA-V model of well-being.

This sixth branch is as important as the other five, because we can only optimally flourish when we're nourished through moving, sleeping, eating and breathing well. After creating, testing and validating a number of interventions online, skilled therapists were given some positive psychotherapy interventions to use face to face with patients diagnosed with severe depression. These exercises – such as self-reflective and interactive gratitude practices, savouring and kindness activities – were tested against cognitive behavioural therapy (CBT) and antidepressants over 14 sessions and, remarkably, the positive psychotherapy interventions – some of which are included in this book – worked better than the usual treatment.

Of course, mediation and traditional psychotherapy – such as talking therapy, psychoanalysis and counselling – still have their place in treating mental illness, managing mental health and reducing that which debilitates life but to enable flourishing, there's more that can be done.

Why does flourishing matter?

Over the past few decades, the world seems to have become increasingly frowny. According to research, despite having so much more freedom, work–life balance and material gains than ever before (we can now instantly shop without leaving our houses), entire nations are generally no happier – and in some cases less happy – than they were 50 years ago before all this convenience made life seemingly "easier". This may be puzzling, but it's no surprise to researchers who found that better external factors (e.g. money, marriage, health) do not make us happier. In fact, all these together generally "account for no more than 15 per cent variance in life satisfaction". This is in line with research by Professor Sonja Lyubomirsky, whose cited 1996 studies of adult twins (which assessed well-being at ten-year intervals) revealed that our circumstances only impact our level of life satisfaction by 10 per cent, compared with the impact of our thoughts, feelings and actions, which contribute approximately 40 per cent (with a proportion down to genetics).

How we *think*, what we *believe*, how we *feel* and what we spend our time *doing* (and who we spend that time with) impacts our mental health far more than our circumstances, so if we can find ways to manage these controllable elements of our life – and learn to respond well with acceptance and compassion to what's outside our control – we can flourish.

As well as equipping ourselves with tools to alleviate anxiety, fight fear or tackle depression, we need tools that don't just work on our weaknesses but help us develop our strengths and amplify what's good. Fundamentally, we need to find balance, which is where the ABC of Flourishing™ – Acceptance, Balance and Compassion – comes in.

Where shall we go?

To create conditions for flourishing in a garden, when you plant a flower in the ground you don't just shove it in the earth – you need to nourish it with nutrients and tend to it; you water the plant and feed it; you keep the area weed free. To flourish, your flower needs favourable conditions and an environment that enables flourishing. We are the same.

You Can Flourish is broken up into three parts – THINK, FEEL and DO, based on the three areas of our lives we have control over, and in which we are able to create those favourable conditions and enabling environment.

In **Part One – Think: Thoughts** we'll explore expectation and perception, because the expectations placed on us and how we see the world have a huge impact on our day-to-day wellness and flourishing capability.

In **Part Two – Feel: Feelings** we'll explore the importance of expression. Uncomfortable emotions can be difficult to express, yet suppression without expression can lead to depression. We'll explore ways to feel it all with compassion.

Finally, in **Part Three – Do: Actions** we'll explore the PERMA-V positive psychology interventions and practical actions that can boost our wellness and help us manage our mental health across the six branches of well-being.

Plus, we'll look at how to find balance between accomplishing all we wish to achieve and being grateful for all we already have, and bring balance into other areas of our lives. You may need a notebook to elaborate on the work you do within this workbook.

Action creates momentum. The more you intentionally do to boost your own well-being, the more you will flourish and the greater positive impact you can have on those around you too. In the garden of life, it's time to flourish.

THE ABC OF FLOURISHING

Nothing ever goes away until it has taught us what we need to know.

Pema Chödrön

As I sit beneath the heavy boughs of an old horse-chestnut tree, I think about what has brought me here – not literally to this location, resting here on this ancient arboreal seat, but how I came to be doing the work I do, writing books to enable flourishing. My thoughts turn to my parents, and I feel a soft tug at my heart, heavy and light in equal measure. Heavy because I wish so hard that they were here – at the other end of a phone, available for a chat or a cuddle; and light because I realize the books I write are a kind of "co-destiny" with them. I likely wouldn't have been so devoted to helping people make sense of life and how to make the most of it had both my parents not lost theirs.

It was the observation about how differently my mum and my dad viewed and responded to life, along with other people's observations about my own optimism and resilience despite my loss, which sparked my interest in positive psychology. My mum, who had multiple sclerosis (MS), was physically disabled yet mentally able – positive and resilient with a sunny smile and confident disposition. My dad was physically able yet mentally unwell. He was diagnosed with manic depression, and beneath his loving heart his head found life a struggle. While Mum coped well with what life threw at her, Dad didn't. But what Dad lacked in positivity, he made up for in his passion for creative pursuits and hobbies (playing guitar, landscape gardening, learning French and dancing).

My mum died when I was 17. She gave me her optimism and zest. My dad died when I was 39. He gave me his creativity and passion. They both gave me enough love to last my own lifetime. Like many who've experienced a traumatic event I somehow managed to grow, perhaps not despite adversity but *because* of it – my perspective and attitude were shaped by loss and longing to make me more appreciative, determined and hopeful.

I was editing my first self-help book when my dad received his terminal asbestosis diagnosis. His death (Dad was 67 when he lost his life, Mum was 43) made me even more determined to provide tools to help people make the most of their lives. Here had been a family of three – all different, yet we each flourished in different ways. You don't just have to think positive or be a high achiever to flourish. Realistic optimism, having hope, doing the best you can with what you have from where you are and working through challenges – that's flourishing.

Since then, I've thought a lot about the pressures of modern life and the impact it has on our capacity to flourish. The pressure on us to be happy, successful, fit and gorgeous is overwhelming. I sometimes joke in workshops – you think *you're* under pressure, imagine being an optimism teacher and well-being author! The expectation of needing to have it all together is strong, but we're all human so we all struggle, and we are all works in progress with our challenges to bear. That's life.

As the wind whispers through the broad leaves above me, I wonder about what gets in the way of flourishing and I jot down a list in my journal.

- Not having time for what and/or who matters most.
- Feeling unseen, unheard or misunderstood.
- Hormonal changes and their effect on mood.
- Berating ourselves for something we've said or done in the past.
- Ruminating on a situation in our present.
- Worrying about what might happen in the future.
- Believing we're not good enough.
- Bottling up emotions behind a brave face.
- Behaving based on how we think we should rather than authentically.
- Comparing ourselves with others without knowing the reality of their actual lives.
- Lack of sleep, exercise or time outdoors in nature.

We want less stress, judgement and regret; and we want more joy, clarity and ease. To flourish, we need to recognize the thieves and givers of joy, and attend to whatever gets in the way of flourishing while also building on what enables it. So, I think, what if we could:

- Make peace with what we've said or done in the past, have compassion for what's happening in the present and build optimism for the future?

- Accept more readily that life can be brutal, people difficult and struggle inevitable?

- Accept the things that cannot be changed and focus on those that can?

- Recognize our strengths rather than focusing on our weaknesses?

What if we could find balance:

- Between busyness and stillness?

- Between the depths of despair and soothing self-care?

- Between numbing screen time and nourishing "green" time?

- Between imagining the worst and expecting the best?

- Between allowing discomfort and savouring delight?

- Between appreciating what we already have and what we hope to get?

- Between accepting who we already are and growing into who we wish to become?

What might this look like and how can we do this step by step? Thankfully, where there are problems and obstacles we can find solutions and opportunities. Following a decade of study, I realize the antidotes to the judgement, worry, trauma and stress of life are:

- Acceptance.

- Balance.

- Compassion.

    +

- PERMA-V interventions.

The ABC of Flourishing™

In addition to the scientifically tested PERMA-V interventions I'd learned about during my positive psychology training, much of what gets in the way of flourishing can be attended to by periodically checking in with ourselves and examining our lives through a lens of acceptance, balance and compassion. For while there is PERMA-V – and the scientifically tested interventions that enable it, covered in Part Three – there is also ABC.

You Can Flourish then is about finding balance in life rather than striving for constant happiness, so we may function optimally. It's about learning to accept our flaws and off days, and developing deeper compassion for ourselves and our fellow beings. Life is heart-breaking *and* heart-warming. The *and* is the equilibrium, where we can find balance and, at times, peace. Our practised acceptance of this *and* – plus the difficult and wonderful extremities of our lived experience – is where we can find compassion and the key to a well-balanced life.

In shifting how we see and respond to the world and ourselves – and by releasing the pressures and expectations that come from both – we can lean into feeling what we feel without shame or blame, and we can live through this lens of greater acceptance, balance and compassion – ABC. And by gradually introducing positive psychology interventions into our daily lives, we can build the foundations of flourishing and live our roller coaster lives fully and well. Are you ready?

Part One

THINK: THOUGHTS

Chapter One
EXPECTATION

GETTING TO KNOW HOW WE THINK

You might think a book about flourishing would focus primarily on positivity, but it's crucial to explore the parts of life and thought processes that generate negativity too. There's a big difference between negative thoughts and negative emotions. The latter are useful parts of what it means to be human. The former, while natural, can be destructive and inaccurate and get in the way of flourishing as they shape how we view and speak to ourselves. It's important to understand what's behind them so we can minimize any damaging impact. Especially given how much our thoughts and beliefs influence our feelings and behaviour – and that bad is stronger than good. We are essentially wired for negativity; pessimism comes more naturally to us than optimism. This is due to our evolutionary inbuilt negativity bias, which was designed to protect us from danger but nowadays can lead to depression and anxiety.

Back when danger and disease lurked around every corner (sabre-toothed tigers, high child mortality rates, low life-expectancy) there were survival advantages to being anxious and judgemental. It was far better to worry about creatures and diseases that could kill us than risk death by ignoring them. But this built-in "harm-alarm" is no longer as fit for purpose as it was.

Thousands of years later, this negativity bias is why newspapers lead with bad news, why we'll focus our attention on the one bad review or result, rather than the 99 good ones, and why our minds automatically focus on the negative rather than the positive by default. It's also why bringing the balance back is so important, why we need to counter this slant toward negative stimuli with intentional interventions that generate positive thoughts and emotions. This doesn't mean we dismiss, ignore or avoid the negative, just that we work on finding a better, less-skewed balance.

First, we need to sort through what's helpful and unhelpful, what's accurate and inaccurate, and which thought processes need the most attention and work. Then we can uncover our own inner truth and become emotionally agile, realistically optimistic – rather than blindly so – and ready to flourish. We need to consider what gets us down if we are going to lift ourselves up. In this chapter we'll shine a light on some of the darker parts of the human experience in terms of how expectations can deflate us and explore what we can do about this.

Recent research suggests humans have 6,000 thoughts per day. That's a lot of thinking! We spend a lot of time in our heads, even when we're busy *doing*. Our thoughts range from the factual "I'm hungry"; to the fantasy "I wonder..."; to the thoughts about what's next "what if...?"; to the judgemental "I/they should have...". The last two types of thoughts warrant the most attention, because "what's next" thoughts can lead to catastrophic thinking, crisis-mongering and anxiety, while judgemental thoughts can lead to helplessness, rumination and depression. We'll focus on those in more detail in Chapter 3.

WHAT IS EXPECTATION?

Expectation is a powerful belief, or set of beliefs, about what we expect life to look like. It's worthy of consideration, because it can lead to both "what's next" and judgemental thoughts when expectations don't match reality. As a form of perception there are two types:

1. What we believe/think/hope/expect to happen in the future.

2. What we expect from others/what we and others expect from ourselves.

Both types can impact our well-being. Indeed, your imagined future – the life you envision for yourself – can have a great effect on your present life, depending on whether your current life aligns with those expectations or not.

It's in our nature to nurture future possibilities. Future prospection – this ability we possess to visualize potential outcomes – is a core part of what it means to be human. Interestingly, the circuit of neurons in our brain that lights up when we're asked to visualize our imagined future is the same one that lights up when we're resting. This "hope circuit" is our default network and it drives much of our behaviour. New research suggests that our sense of agency about the future may even drive our present behaviour as much as our past experiences do. This means therapists can uncover a lot by exploring clients' expectations as well as their past traumas.

Exploring expectation is important because we don't always get what we want in life. Dreams are dashed and expectations unmet. This truth impacts how we think, feel and show up in our daily lives, creating disappointment, disharmony and discombobulation.

A word about disappointment and regret

Disappointment and regret, along with love and shame, are some of the most commonly felt emotions. They can be exhausting too, taking their toll both on our relationships with others and our relationship with ourselves. Yet, like most of our so-called "negative" emotions, disappointment – like its sibling regret – has much to teach us. If used wisely, disappointment and regret can help us make better decisions, deepen our sense of meaning and improve our performance.

Both disappointment and regret are generated when things don't go according to plan. The former tends to arise when we don't see ourselves as the cause of the outcome, whereas the latter tends to come from the belief that we are the cause of something. We'll regret what we have or haven't done or said, the opportunities missed, the chances blown, the action not taken.

Finding the good in the bad

Indeed, there is richness in "negative" emotions, as we'll explore in Chapter 3. Take boredom, for example. Being bored is seen as a negative feeling that can cause irritability, frustration and lethargy. It's the opposite of feeling engaged, challenged and motivated – and, when bored, we're more likely to numb than nourish ourselves. Yet, boredom can also lead to productive outcomes. When a child (or indeed an adult) is bored, they might pick up a guitar or a book and become inspired to write a song or a story. Mundanity can inspire creativity. A lack of stimulation can give imagination space to daydream, play and create. In accepting that feeling of boredom, we can welcome space for something good.

Similarly, regret, which can lead to uncomfortable feelings of blame and shame, does have its uses. As American author Daniel Pink says in *The Power of Regret: How Looking Backward Moves Us Forward*, "When people tell you what they regret in life they are telling you what they value in life."

While boredom is a call for imagination, regret is a call for change. Research professor and author Brené Brown says, "No regrets doesn't mean living with courage, it means living without reflection." Reflection is vital to flourishing. I have plenty of regrets. Although we were close, I wish I'd spent more time with my mum and asked her more questions about her life, thoughts and dreams. I regret not going to Bournemouth University when my boyfriend at the time said he'd dump me if I did (I was scared to lose him having lost my mum while I was at college, but now I know better). And I regret turning down an invitation to the press launch of *We Will Rock You* because I didn't realize Robert De Niro was going to be there. I could've been in the same room as the actual Robert. De. Niro. Multiple face palms!

Regrets can lead us to feel guilty (more on that emotion later), but they can also be useful. They can give us clues, hope and hindsight. What would we have done differently if we knew then what we know now? That's a question worthy of reflection that can generate life-enhancing answers. Regrets about missed opportunities have taught me to seize current opportunities. Regrets about things I wish I'd said have taught me to say what matters to who matters. Regrets about not asking enough questions have taught me to be curious and ask those darn questions!

STEP 1: Reflect on regret

Write down some of your own regrets. What are you disappointed about? (Things that you aren't responsible for.) What are your biggest regrets? (Things you feel responsible for.) What are your "If only I hads/hadn'ts"?

If only I had/hadn't ....

....

....

....

What have they taught you? ....

....

....

....

What fundamental needs, wants and values do they reveal about what matters most to you?

....

....

....

What can you do differently today/tomorrow as a result of what you wish you'd done yesterday?

....

....

....

How might you speak to a best friend who shared this regret with you? What would you say to them?

....

....

....

Where do our expectations come from?

Oddly, many of our expectations and other beliefs don't even come from us – they come from inherited ideals about what society, parents, peers and the media say we *should* do, be or have. External expectations can hijack our authentic belief systems. I call these conditioned social norms around what is expected of us the "shackles of should", as they are often restrictive, frequently unhelpful and sometimes even harmful. Releasing these shackles is freeing.

Take, for example, the limiting expectations around gender where men are expected to be strong and avoid showing emotion, weakness or vulnerability, despite suppression of emotion being detrimental to mental and physical health. While women are still expected to meet restrictive ideals around beauty: to stay slim, look young and sexy, yet avoid "provoking" undesirable actions from men. The social conditioning of "shoulds" starts young and leads girls to underestimate their strength and abilities, and boys to overestimate theirs. Restrictive societal "shoulds" extend to what toys, colours and motifs boys and girls *should* prefer, preventing kids from feeling comfortable enough to be themselves, which is carried on through to adulthood.

It's not just children who are bombarded with "shoulds". Parents today are expected to raise children to be healthy-eating, emotionally well-balanced, well-behaved, extra-curricular-activity-pursuing academic high achievers – i.e. perfect, which is unrealistic and piles too much pressure on parent and child alike.

SUCCESS AND SELF-WORTH

Expectations around success are deeply ingrained. In our meritocratic society we are assessed, graded and compared constantly from an early age. From how soon we take our first step and reach key developmental milestones to how rapidly we climb the career ladder and accumulate status symbols that signal our success – all for the approval of, first, our parents, then our peers and wider society. But what about ourselves?

External approval matters because belonging and social acceptance are evolutionary requirements of survival. Back in our cave-dwelling days anything that might result in ejection from the safety of the tribe was bad, so our human need for acceptance and approval is wired in. We consequently seek to impress, and success is deemed good, while failure is bad. How ironic that most successful people have failed first and attribute much of their success to learning from mistakes made on the way. Perfectionists are less likely to take risks or try something out for fear of failure, which ironically hampers chances of success or "perfection". Yet the importance of failure is not a narrative we are taught.

So, we people-please for approval – a natural tendency that starts as soon as we say "look at me!" to parents to glean praise. Having an absent parent or a dismissive one, or growing up in a house with conflict, can take our people-pleasing to a higher level as we seek to prove ourselves.
In *David and Goliath: Underdogs, Misfits and the Art of Battling Giants*, Malcolm Gladwell states that parental loss often dictates a higher-than-average ambition level, especially for "eminent orphans" who lost a parent

before they turned 18. I have always put my own ambition down to my mum's loving encouragement, but her death did make me want to prove that her belief in me was right. The point is, we aim to please, driven by the question: "What will people think?". Approval is vital for our survival, but it's made us dislike uncertainty, failure, rejection and discomfort. Yet, some uncertainty in life *is* certain. Failure and rejection are par for the course (and oh-so useful), and discomfort is an inevitable and inescapable part of being human.

The realization that many of our expectations and other beliefs are external demonstrates the importance of questioning our conditioning periodically, to check in with our own personal truth so we can release the "shackles of should" and discover who we truly are underneath these layers of expectation.

STEP 2: Expectation inventory: take stock of your "shoulds"

Think about what you expect your life to be like and what you expect of yourself (e.g. what you should look like, be doing career-wise, how you should feel, what you should have achieved, what you should own, and so on). List as many expectations as you can.

I should: ....

....

....

....

Next list your roles in life, such as parent, daughter/son, sibling, friend, occupation, and so on. Next to the role, write down the general expectations of what good performance in that role looks like:

....

....

....

....

....

Consider where or who these expectations have come from. Social media? Society? Parents? Peers? Your partner? Your boss?

....

....

....

....

- Tick those that feel reasonable – for example, that your boss expects you to be punctual.

- Put a cross next to those that feel unreasonable or unrealistic.

- Put a cross next to those that don't honour your true authentic self or restrict you in other ways, preventing you from doing what matters most to you.

Write here which of these "shackles of should" you'd like to break free from and how you might do so:

....

....

....

....

....

STEP 3: Ramp up your self-acceptance, appreciation and compassion

Our self-perception is often skewed. According to research by Cornell University, we significantly over-think our social blunders, overestimate how much of what we do is noticed by others and underestimate how liked we are. This miscalculation of what others think of us is called "the liking gap". By focusing on celebrating and accepting both our strengths and weaknesses we can counter this skewed self-perception.

Know your strengths. Complete the Values in Action (VIA) survey (viacharacter.org) to discover your top character strengths and consider ways to use them regularly. Write your top three here:

....

....

Create a piece of word art or calligraphy listing your top strengths, and put it somewhere you'll see it often.

Know your worth. List two obstacles you've overcome. What was the problem or challenge and how did you resolve it/cope?

....

....

What superpowers did you use?

....

....

Write down positive messages you've received from others. You don't need to believe them yet, write them down anyway. Seven things I want to celebrate about myself are:

....

....

....

....

....

....

....

List your achievements as far back as you can. A medal for netball when you were ten? Getting *that* job? Having the courage to leave a job or leaving a toxic relationship?

....

....

....

....

Now write down what you think are your weaknesses. (You may have been told and/or believe you are "too" this or "not enough", for example.) Here are mine: I am messy, forgetful, impatient, too sensitive, too talkative, too enthusiastic, too independent, I try too hard and I'm not tidy enough...

....

....

....

....

Would your loved ones still love you despite this evidence of your human-ness? As the most enduring relationship we have is with ourselves, can you soften into doing so too? That's self-compassion. Appreciate the beauty of these imperfections. Find the good in your quirks. For example, I'm naturally messy so it takes effort to be tidy – but messiness equals freedom from perfectionism. Being "too sensitive" means I notice important things that others may not. As Glennon Doyle says, "The opposite of sensitive is not brave, it's insensitive, and that's no badge of honour." Write down a positive benefit that comes from perceived "weaknesses":

....

....

....

....

Accept where you currently are and that this is where you are meant to be. Then consider how you might move forward and progress. That's active acceptance rather than passive acceptance.

Write a thank-you note to yourself. While you're doubting yourself, someone else is admiring you. So, take a moment to see yourself in a better light. Thank yourself for being you, for overcoming specific challenges using certain strengths. Acknowledge these and resolve to use them in the future. Thank yourself for positively impacting the world around you and jot down how you do so. Remind yourself that you're stronger than you thought you were and that your weaknesses are what make you human; resolve to keep being you and to give yourself a break. Sign off with love.

....

....

....

....

....

EXPECTATIONS OF OTHERS

Expecting so much from other people can create disappointment and disharmony, and can have a negative effect on our relationships. Focusing on what disappoints us about each other is not nurturing or connective. Plus, where do these expectations come from?

Our expectations of others can be deeply rooted in our own experiences that have nothing to do with those we're expecting something from. For example, if you had an absent parent, you might expect your partner to be what that parent wasn't; or, if your parents were encouraging, you might expect the same level of encouragement from your partner. However, that's unreasonable as it's not their job to be what your parent was or wasn't. It's their job to be themselves. We can't change someone to fit our expectations of them, just as they cannot change us to fit theirs. Truth bomb: other people weren't born to be who you expect them to be, nor to behave a certain way just so you can feel good about yourself.

Equally, we might expect of our children what our parents expected of us; or we might expect them to be more like us despite them growing up in a different world. We need to remind ourselves not to put unreasonable expectations on our children; to allow them to develop their own unique strengths and become all that they are. Comparing a child with the high-achieving super-sporty seemingly well-behaved children we see on social media is no more helpful than comparing ourselves with our own peers. It gets in the way of authenticity and it can be harmful to the person we're expecting so much from and our relationship with them. What if we shifted our focus from what they are *not* doing or who they are *not* being, to instead accept and appreciate what they *are* doing and who they truly are?

STEP 4: Take stock of your expectations of others

Write down what you expect from others and consider where those expectations came from:

I expect my family to: ....

I expect my partner to: ....

I expect my friends to: ....

I expect my boss/work colleagues to: ....

Where have these expectations come from? ....

Are these expectations reasonable? ....

Are any based on fulfilling your own need to feel good about yourself (as a parent/son/daughter/sibling/friend/manager/worker)?

....

Do these expectations enable people to be their authentic selves?

....

Are they aware of these expectations? Have you expressed them?

....

EXPRESSION OF EXPECTATIONS

During extensive research into human emotion, Brené Brown uncovered two types of expectation: examined/expressed expectations and stealth or unexamined/unexpressed expectations. The latter have more of a negative impact on our lives. Conversely, by examining and expressing expectations with the people in our lives, we can minimize the damage they inflict. While you and those involved in co-creating your experiences may have different ideas about what your ideal weekend/holiday/home/ life might look like, you most likely have a shared intention – to make your time together enjoyable. Mutually exploring expectations to find common ground can reduce the chances of disappointment. You could:

- Share your expectations with those you are expecting something from. What do you want and why? This can help minimize blame, shame, frustrations and disappointment down the line.

- Invite others to share their expectations with you. What do they want and why does this matter to them?

- Reality-check your/their expectations. Are there any that rely on something outside of your control that you can let go of, such as other people's responses or the weather?

Sometimes our own expectations are influenced by what everyone else is doing. We want our life to measure up to theirs even though we know we are comparing our blooper reel with everyone else's show reel and never ever know the full story. We know comparison is futile, yet we still do it. Because meritocratic society has conditioned us to measure ourselves against each other, we yearn to be one of life's winners. We don't want to fail despite failure's usefulness; and we avoid loss, despite it being part of life – loss of loved ones, pets, relationships, jobs, opportunities and, of course, the loss of life turning out how we'd hoped. Yet loss is rarely normalized – society and media sell us the gloss not the loss, perpetuating the myth that everyone else has it all together and is living a better life.

The truth is, however, that they don't and they're not. Everyone is fighting some kind of battle we likely know nothing about. We don't see each other's pain because we're conditioned to put on a brave face. We have no idea what the people we pass in the street are going through. The person with the loving husband and amazing children might be battling mental or physical health issues. The high achiever might be struggling in their relationship. Susan Cain, author of *Bittersweet: How Sorrow and Longing Make Us Whole*, told me that imagining captions floating above the person at the checkout or in the supermarket queue, illustrating what might be going on in their lives, can make us more open to what they might be dealing with.

Acknowledging our mutual inevitable suffering reminds us of our common humanity, which is one way to strengthen our compassion for others and ourselves, according to Kristin Neff, author of *Self-Compassion: The Proven Power of Being Kind to Yourself*. Because nobody has it all together and we truly are in this together. So, how can we better respond?

STEP 5: Add compassion to the comparison mix

To reduce the negative impact of comparison, we need to bring compassion for others and ourselves into our comparative experience. You could try:

- Wishing people well when you find you are comparing yourself to them. Brené Brown says she does this when she is swimming and finds herself comparing her pace to the person in the next lane. She says in her head, "Have a great swim."

- Reminding yourself your value doesn't come from your bank balance, job title or productivity output, because you're not a machine. Your value comes from whether you made someone smile today, whether your choices were aligned with your values (see page 110) and whether are you being yourself. Don't dilute yourself. You deserve to be full-strength YOU!

Write down alternative ways you might value your own self-worth that aren't influenced by the "shackles of should":

....

....

....

STEP 6: Harness the power of envy as a self-improvement tool

When someone else has something we want, we can feel envy. Whether it's related to their lifestyle, intelligence, popularity, looks, status or wealth, it tends to flare up in areas of life we feel are out of synch with our expectations. The "love my work" post when you hate your job; the "married my best friend" post when you feel incompatible with your partner; the endless stream of baby pics when you're struggling to conceive or are grieving for your angel baby; the "proud mumma" images when you're concerned about your teen's (quite normal) lack of motivation.

Envy highlights areas where you may need to process your emotions to find a way forward and highlights scope for meaningful changes (e.g. find a new job, work on a relationship or let it go). Like inspiration, envy tells us in no uncertain terms what we desire. Thank you, envy. What if, rather than seething with envy, we harnessed the power of it to take positive action and move our lives in the direction we desire?

WHAT GENERATES ENVY AND INSPIRATION IN YOU?

Which people, places, achievements, lifestyles, relationships, jobs, style or character traits are you envious of and/or inspired by?

....

....

....

Revisit this data when plotting your goals on pages 122–5.

I'LL BE HAPPY WHEN...

Expectations tend to be driven by what we actually want – as our disappointment, envy and inspiration show us – and what we are told we *should* want, e.g. success and happiness. We are mis-sold the myth that success and wealth lead to fulfillment. So, we tie our happiness to a future achievement or purchase, thinking, "I'll be happy when... I have more money, live in my dream home, drive a better car, buy those sparkly new shoes, get that promotion, achieve that goal, prove myself to my parents..."

The truth is, you won't, or at least not for as long as you might hope. There is a low correlation between wealth and happiness. How much money we have and how much stuff we own makes little difference to our joy levels once our basic needs of food and shelter have been met. External factors do not make us *lastingly* happier, unless they give our life meaning. To better understand this, it's worth mentioning the two key concepts of happiness in psychology: eudemonic happiness comes from experiences of meaning and purpose (hence the inclusion of "meaning" in PERMA-V) while hedonic happiness comes from the experiences of pleasure and enjoyment (positive emotion). We need both to flourish, but eudemonic happiness is more predictive of life satisfaction and well-being over the longer term (i.e. it lasts longer).

ANTICIPATION OVER DESTINATION

This is important to know because we consistently overestimate how much positive emotion something will bring and how long it will last. While small accomplishments and retail therapy can temporarily create a spike in satisfaction levels, the novelty soon wears off because of adaption. Humans adapt very quickly to good or bad fortune. Whether we fall in or out of love, get or leave a dream job or win or lose a fortune, after the initial euphoria of the "honeymoon period" (or the pain of the loss) has worn off, we return very quickly to our previous level of life satisfaction. This was proven by studies on lottery winners who were happier for a few months following their good fortune, yet soon returned to their habitual happiness levels, which psychologists call our "set-point".

The mistaken belief of "I'll be happy when..." is called "arrival fallacy" or "summit syndrome". Because arriving at the summit doesn't make us as happy as we expect, it is the thrill of the chase that lights us up; the anticipation of achievement gives us a hit of dopamine from our brain's reward centre. Once we get what we want, the dopamine decreases. Before long we want another shot of that momentary pleasure. This is what keeps us on what psychologists call "the hedonic treadmill", a perpetual strive-win-slump-repeat wheel of constantly wanting more.

If only we could see that the pursuit of the goal makes us feel better than achieving it and devoted more time to enjoying the journey than postponing our happiness until we arrive at our destination. However, thanks to our conditioning, all we can see are the neon lights with arrows pointing to the place we want to get to. This doesn't mean we should stop striving to accomplish goals – quite the contrary. Biologically we are meant to pursue goals, as growth is healthy and rewarding; it's what drives us and gives our lives meaning. Plants can't flourish if they remain as seeds; they need to grow. Growth is the reward, rather than the flower, which only temporarily blooms and doesn't last. Realizing this can be freeing.

Happiness is neither virtue nor pleasure nor this thing nor that, but simply growth. We are happy when we are growing.

W. B. Yeats

STEP 7: Balance work, rest and play

Another myth is that rest equals slacking. We've been conditioned to believe we must work long hours to achieve success. So, we overestimate how much work we can cope with and underestimate how much rest we need. The truth is, effort is rewarding and hard work can often pay off, but only with adequate rest. Long hours are counter-productive and don't deliver results. In fact, working too hard can cause fatigue, affect judgement and even shorten lifespan. Rest enhances performance – it's restorative and productive. Many a scientific breakthrough, or great piece of art or music, came from stopping work and playing, going fishing or sleeping and dreaming.

Swedish psychologist Anders Ericsson's 1993 study of violinists told us that it takes 10,000 hours of practice to become an expert. And yes, practice is effective. However, the less widely reported part of that study is that, while those world-class violin students did practise more purposefully (for 10,000 hours) than their classmates, they also got more rest and slept for 1 hour per day more than the average violin student. Finding a healthy work–life balance is a more fruitful way to live if you want to flourish. Balancing work, rest and play really is the way.

- Reframe rest and play to see them as productive activities. Microsoft Japan trialled a four-day week for staff in 2019 and recorded a 40 per cent increase in productivity after just one month.

- Actively schedule rest and play alongside work. Use different coloured pens for work, rest and play on your calendar so you can see at a glance when you are out of balance.

STEP 8: Define "enoughness"

Define what "good enough" looks like to you and step off the hedonic treadmill.

Ponder on how "less is more" and what that could look like for you. Write down how much more "less" could give you. For example, less work = more rest. Less stuff = more space. Less responsibility = more time. Also flip this to see how more good stuff can minimize the negative. For example, more focus = less distraction and more woodland walks = less stress. Finding balance is often good enough.

Less .... = More ....

Less .... = More ....

Less .... = More ....

More .... = Less ....

More .... = Less ....

More .... = Less ....

Chapter Two

HOPE
AND
OPTIMISM

If high expectations create disappointment, shouldn't we just lower our expectations and be happy when things turn out better than expected? Not necessarily. Expecting less doesn't mean you'll feel less disappointment if your expectations aren't met. Hope and optimism are useful tools in countering the difficult judgements and feelings generated by unmet expectations and are good for both physical and mental health. Envisioning the future, we can either take an optimistic outlook or expect the worst. We can't predict the future, so we may as well take a hopeful view.

Having hope in our hearts and optimism in our minds doesn't just help boost our enjoyment of the present, it also means we are *more likely* to achieve our goals. Multiple studies show that hopeful people flourish more; they perform better and achieve more across academia, sports, political and military domains, even when their abilities are equal with less hopeful people.

Here's why: When hopeful and optimistic, your brain actually performs better and thinks more clearly because you are:

- More open to opportunities, to trying and to taking risks. Hopeful, optimistic people don't fear failure in the way that perfectionists or pessimists do. They anticipate that obstacles occur and accept adversity as par for the course, so tend to be open to accepting challenges and learning from mistakes. This open mindset equips them to deal with difficulties, seize opportunities and see possibilities.

- Better able to problem-solve. Professor Barbara Fredrickson's "broaden-and-build" theory found that a positive mindset expands cognitive functionality and opens the mind to creative ideas and potential solutions, whereas negative thoughts and unhelpful emotions close the logical mind and get stuck in emotional mud.

- Better able to cope with setbacks, challenges and changes. Optimists not only adapt better to negative events and learn lessons from negative experiences, they also tend to be more persistent and active in the face of setbacks. Whereas pessimists tend to give up more readily, generating inertia rather than action. Furthermore, in addition to improving our brain's functionality, Fredrickson also discovered that hope comes into its own during times of crisis. The mental reserve of positivity acts like a currency for you to save up, draw upon and cash in during tough times, making you more resilient. This "build" part of her broaden-and-build theory means you can bounce back from disappointment, guilt, regret and those emotions fuelled by unmet expectations.

BALANCED POSITIVITY AND NEGATIVITY

This evidence for the power of positivity is important to acknowledge, but so is the notion of the "tyranny of positivity" or "toxic positivity". These terms refer to an unhealthy obsession with happiness where pressure to remain positive can make us feel worse. Actively hiding, ignoring or dismissing difficult feelings, painful emotions and problems in favour of staying positive stemmed from the positive mental attitude (PMA) movement. This has left people thinking there's something wrong with them if they experience negative thoughts or emotions and promotes the idea that negativity should be avoided or ignored rather than felt and explored.

Flourishing is about finding balance and a way through, not around. Positivity and negativity are not good versus bad; they are more complex than that. Too much positivity at the expense of *allowing* negativity can be detrimental, just as too much negativity at the expense of *building* positivity can be too. We need negative emotions to act as guides and bridges to connection. But pessimism can be damaging to well-being, as can inaccurate negative thoughts and spirals.

Suppression of negativity is important to acknowledge and address, as we'll explore later – but we must also acknowledge the huge impact of optimism and hope on health. There is no such thing as being too positive, as long as you acknowledge, validate and express negative emotions too. Balance is essential. And, importantly, because humans have a default bias making negativity much easier than positivity, we need to work on the latter, to find a healthy balance between the two.

The following pages focus on building hope and optimism – tackling inaccurate negative beliefs and expressing rather than suppressing so-called "negative" emotions – and aim to help you find that balance.

*The grand essentials to happiness in
this life are something to do, something to
love, and something to hope for.*

Joseph Addison

Mentally, those with high levels of hope score better in life satisfaction and self-esteem studies. A research study on adolescents "found hopefulness to be predictive of subjective well-being, self-esteem and academic adjustment". Optimists and those measuring high on the hope scale have greater self-belief in their problem-solving capabilities and ability to effect change. Consequently, optimists are less likely to suffer from anxiety or depression.

Optimism is not just good for the head, but the heart too. A 2015 report in the *BMC Cardiovascular Disorders* journal found that optimists are at lower risk of coronary heart disease and stroke, and the protective effects of optimism on the human body are claimed to be even greater than those experienced when stopping smoking. Meanwhile, measuring cortisol response, a sign of heart health, an Iranian study of 69 coronary patients found those who were given six weeks of positive psychology interventions had a better cortisol response and lower stress levels 15 weeks later compared with a control group that had no interventions. Studies also show those with high levels of hope are better able to withstand physical pain and recover faster from injury. Optimism and hope can protect us from disease to a certain extent and help us heal faster if we do fall ill. We fare better and protect ourselves from emotional and physical harm by having a hopeful view and optimistic outlook. Evidently, optimism is worth working on.

What's the difference between hope and optimism?

Hope is the bridge between the impossible and the possible.

Joseph Bellezzo

Neither hope nor optimism is a belief that a bright future is guaranteed. Hope means you believe in the best outcome being *possible*. Optimism means you believe in the best outcome being *probable*.

Optimism is (as defined by leading positive psychology professor Ilona Boniwell) "a generalized sense of confidence about the future, characterized by a broad expectancy that outcomes are likely to be positive".

Hope is the belief that you can "get there from here". Whether "here" is amid tragedy and struggle or whether "here" is a place of contentment, having hope is to believe that things can change for the better and you have an active role in the potentiality of the future. It's not just the expectation that the future will be bright; it's the acknowledgement of our participation and ability in making it so. Hope is expectation with action. As such, rather than lowering our expectations to create greater life satisfaction, hope is the key to managing expectations in a healthy way.

STEP 9: Measure your hopes

By working on our perception and response we can cultivate more hope and turn pessimism into optimism – but first, measure how hopeful you are using Penn University's Future Scale (also known as the Trait Hope Scale).

Read each of the 12 items below carefully. Using the scale (1–8) below, select the number that best describes you and put that number in the blank provided.

1 = Definitely false

2 = Mostly false

3 = Somewhat false

4 = Slightly false

5 = Slightly true

6 = Somewhat true

7 = Mostly true

8 = Definitely true

1. I can think of many ways to get out of a jam. ....

2. I energetically pursue my goals. ....

3. I feel tired most of the time. ....

4. There are lots of ways around any problem. ....

5. I am easily downed in an argument. ....

6. I can think of many ways to get the things in life that are important to me. ....

7. I worry about my health. ....

8. Even when others get discouraged, I know I can find a way to solve the problem. ....

9. My past experiences have prepared me well for my future. ....

10. I've been pretty successful in life. ....

11. I usually find myself worrying about something. ....

12. I meet the goals that I set for myself. ....

Scoring your future scale:

To find your agency subscale score, add together your answers for questions 2, 9, 10 and 12.

To find your pathway subscale score, add together your answers for questions 1, 4, 6 and 8.

To find your total Trait Hope Scale score, add your agency and pathway scores together. If you score below 24, you have lower than average hope, and if you score 24 or higher you are generally hopeful.

THE IMPORTANCE OF PERCEPTION

To have high hope we need to be able to clearly define *what* we want to achieve (goals) and *how* we intend to achieve them (pathways), then be sufficiently motivated to take the necessary steps to do so (agency).

In 1995, the world's first hope scientist Rick Snyder focused on our perception that we can generate effective pathways to accomplish desired goals and have the mental energy to believe, "I can do this" and "I will get this done". All of this comes down to self-perception. It's time to consider how we view ourselves and our world.

Chapter Three
PERCEPTION AND RESPONSE

The lens through which we see the world is crucial to flourishing because our perception guides our response – how we think impacts how we feel and what we do. We can split perception into three parts – expectation, interpretation and attribution.

Our expectations are about what we think will happen. Our interpretation is how we explain to ourselves what is happening. Our attribution is how we explain to ourselves why it's happening.

An example of the attribution part of our perception is known as our "explanatory style", which is how we habitually perceive and explain the cause of why something good or bad has happened to us; where we attribute credit or blame for good or bad events (personalization), whether we perceive them as impacting other areas of our lives (pervasiveness) and for how long those effects may last (permanence). As Professor Seligman explains, "the basis of optimism does not lie in positive phrases or images of victory, but in the way you think about causes."

EXPLANATORY STYLE

Our explanatory thinking style affects how we feel about and thus how we respond to setbacks and successes in terms of the choices and decisions we make – all of which impacts whether we flourish or languish. Optimistic and pessimistic thinkers will explain the cause of an event differently based on one or more of "three Ps": personalization, permanence and pervasiveness.

Same event, different response

Let's say two people try out for the football team but neither is selected. The pessimist might say, "I'm always bad at passing and I'm such a terrible player. I'm never going to be good enough for the team. What's the point? I give up." (Personalization, i.e. it's all my fault; and permanence, i.e. it's always bad, never good.) Whereas the optimist might say, "I didn't pass the ball well this time. I just need to practise my passing skills and try again." (Personalization, i.e. controllable and therefore changeable; permanence, i.e. temporary and workable.) The same event happened to both the optimist and the pessimist, but one will have another shot, opting to try again with more effort. The other has closed the door on that opportunity and decided to stop altogether. The same event, two thinking styles, two different types of behaviour that result in two different outcomes – one life-enhancing and one life-diminishing.

Based on the three Ps, if they *had* made the team, the optimist would likely attribute the success to their own efforts and see it as sustainable long-term, while the pessimist would likely see it as a lucky fluke that won't last.

These thinking styles are powerful because they can create self-fulfilling prophecies. For example, if you believe you can make the team next time by practising more, you'll improve your skills and likely get selected, proving yourself right – "I can!" But the same is true if you give up in the face of setbacks. Quitting makes you less likely to be selected. Your belief that you're not good enough will be proved right too. "See, I knew I wasn't good enough" – perpetuating the pessimistic thoughts "I can't do this", "I'll never be good enough" and "I always mess up".

Pessimists are more likely to churn over these unhelpful thoughts and get stuck in rumination – an easy place to get stuck – which makes a pessimist feel even worse. Thankfully, pessimism is not a trait, it has been learned, which means it can be unlearned and updated. We can learn optimism by examining our thoughts and beliefs.

WHAT'S IN A BELIEF?

Our beliefs (interpretations, attributions and expectations) tend to be based on either "judgemental" thoughts or "what's next" thoughts. "Judgemental" thoughts are based on how we interpret or attribute meaning to something, while "what's next" thoughts can be expectations or worries. Left unchecked, the former can lead to depression while the latter can lead to anxiety. Now, it's important to remember that thoughts are simply neurons firing; they are not facts. And beliefs are simply neural networks of thoughts we've repeated often – a cocktail of judgements, opinions, memories, predictions and worries. The more we repeat a thought, the stronger the neural network becomes. This is important because we make sense of the world through these neural narratives.

Whose belief is it anyway?

As we've learned, many stories we tell ourselves originated from other people – thoughts we've internalized, repeated and turned into beliefs, despite them being fictitious rather than factual narratives. For example, the belief, "I'm no artist, I'm terrible at art" may have been "written" into a neural network after a teacher criticized your artwork as a child. What if the teacher was having a terrible day and was preoccupied about a situation at home? You didn't know that, so you internalized their story about your art capabilities as your own narrative. Or perhaps you believe someone doesn't like you because of the way they look at you, but you just remind them of someone who was mean to them, and it has nothing to do with you?

Thanks to the neuroplasticity of our wonderful brains we can form new neural connections. This is more difficult when depressed because neuroplasticity decreases, so our thinking patterns can become less flexible and more fixed. Antidepressants (medicinal and nature's antidepressants – nature and exercise) along with talking therapies, such as CBT, work to form new neural connections and reinstate neuroplasticity to its former capability.

The malleability of our brains means we can change our beliefs by questioning our thoughts and repeating different ones to carve out new neural pathways. Psychologists call this reframing and it involves replacing inaccurate, inflexible and unhelpful thoughts with more accurate, flexible and helpful ones that better serve us. Put simply, if we can change our stories, we can change our lives.

STEP 10: Build thought awareness

Because of this relationship between thoughts, feelings and actions, it's possible to shift your life experience by shifting your life beliefs. To access your beliefs, you need to notice and note down your thoughts about a situation (adversity). You can do this either by observing your mind-chatter in real time (which can be difficult) or you can reflect on your thoughts/ feelings and actions about a previous activating event, i.e. the situation that activated your mind-chatter.

This practice of putting the thinker back in charge of the thought is what psychologists call "metacognition" – thinking about what we're thinking, paying attention to our attention. Noticing thoughts then observing the feelings they induce and even saying "stop" when you notice yourself ruminating is a method that puts you back in control. Rather than go straight into challenging and reframing our beliefs, the first step is awareness. Have a go with this exercise:

A – activating event
Explain an adversity. What is the negative event/situation/circumstance? e.g. He criticized my work again.

Write your own here: ....

....

B – belief
What are your thoughts and beliefs about this adversity? *Why* do you think this has happened? e.g. I'm always messing up under pressure. He'll probably fire me.

Write your own here: ....

....

C – consequence
How did/does this experience make you feel? e.g. I feel disappointed, annoyed, frustrated, embarrassed.

I feel ....

....

How did this feeling make you respond/act/behave as a result? e.g. I didn't go into work and have lost confidence. I might resign.

....

....

What if the criticism was constructive and given because he believes in and champions you? If you take it on board, you might be rewarded. You can only change this belief if you question it. After getting to know your beliefs and how they impact your behaviour, you can work on reframing and replacing unhelpful thoughts to become more accurate. After all, if we're going to base our actual self-worth on our thoughts and beliefs and make life-enhancing or life-diminishing choices based on them, we may as well ensure they're as accurate as possible.

Generating more realistic, flexible and helpful thoughts involves reframing our judgemental thoughts and getting perspective to stop our worried "what's next" thoughts from spiralling out of control. We can do this by finding evidence to dispute unhelpful thoughts and support more accurate alternatives.

STEP 11: Take your thoughts to court

Don't think about a blue elephant.

It's highly likely that you did think about a blue elephant. Trying not to think a thought doesn't work. If you try to force an unhelpful thought or belief out of your head, it will soon pop up again, because it needs to be dealt with. It's like pushing a beach ball under water – it'll soon pop up to the surface. The only way to get rid of that beach ball is to pop it. And the only way to get rid of that thought bubble is to pop it, then you can replace it with a new, more helpful one. Here's how:

- Identify the thought and whether it is helpful/life-enhancing or unhelpful/life-diminishing. Is it helping you show up in the world as you want to? Ask yourself:
  - Does this thought serve me?
  - Does it help me achieve my goal?
  - Does it help me feel how I want to feel?

  For example, if thinking "I'm not going to do well in this test" means you will feel motivated to revise and work harder to achieve the result you want, it could serve you. But if it makes you feel worried and stressed out, preventing action, it is not serving you.

- Dispute those unhelpful thoughts with evidence to the contrary. Can you know with certainty that this thought is true? Fact-check to provide evidence against that thought. What other factors might be contributing to this outcome? Use the following prefixes to reframe:

- This is not true because... (e.g. I've revised as much as I can and chances are I'll do OK).

  - Another way of seeing that is... (e.g. I'm just feeling nervous, which is normal. I can only do my best).

- Consider whether the degree of emotional judgement is justified. For example, at one end of the spectrum is high emotion, "I'm *always* messing up"; versus low emotion, "I *never* mess up" at the other end. Often the middle is truest – i.e. "I *sometimes* mess up."

- Reframe unhelpful thoughts into more helpful, accurate and flexible ones, using the evidence you've uncovered.

Belief	Evidence
Belief identified for reframe.	That's not true because... /Another way of seeing that is...
I'm a bad mum. I'm not strict enough.	I'm loving, supportive and encouraging. I try my best to balance discipline with compassion for my child's needs. Nobody gets it right every time.
I'm always messing up at work.	Recently a few things in a row haven't gone to plan, but I get a lot of things right and do a lot of things well. I just forget those.
She doesn't like me any more. She never replies to my messages.	She's busy and she *does* reply when she wants to meet up. She wouldn't want to meet up if she didn't like me.

Evaluate this new thought's accuracy. It's important to ensure you're not replacing a wildly inaccurate negative statement with a wildly inaccurate positive one. For example, going from "I'm terrible at painting" to "I'm the best artist in town" is still inaccurate. A more valid reframe would be, "Painting isn't a strength, but I'm improving with practice."

Now it's your turn:

Belief	Evidence
Belief identified for reframe.	That's not true because.../Another way of seeing that is...

DEALING WITH WORRIES

*I have spent most of my life worrying
about things that have never happened.*

Mark Twain

It's human nature to have "what's next" thoughts about "what ifs". However, based on our evolutionary survival strategy of imagining potential dangers, our protective survival instinct generates worst possible outcomes so we may avoid them. Yet worries don't protect us as much as they intend. Apart from stopping us stepping in front of a moving car or doing something genuinely dangerous, worries are not helpful in our daily lives, especially given the unlikelihood of the imagined dangers they produce.

What's more, our worries start small but can grow, like a snowball rolling downhill, with each thought building on the last, leading to catastrophic thinking spirals. For example, "What if I fail this test? I'll never get into university... My parents will disown me... I'll never achieve anything worthwhile... I'll fail at life." Your brain doesn't go straight from "What if I fail this test?" to "I'll fail at life". It builds from one thought to the next gradually, which tricks us into believing our catastrophic worries are rational thoughts. In reality, they are speculations based on false assumptions with no real content whatsoever.

Another reason irrational thoughts feel accurate is because the brain doesn't recognize the difference between what it sees and what it thinks about. All this doom when you haven't even taken the test yet. And, even if you did fail, you might be able to retake it, or end up working in a job you love that didn't require a degree and is completely unrelated to that test. Anxiety hinders us, so how can we stop the snowball in its tracks? By getting some perspective.

STEP 12: Find balance and gain perspective

Worries are thoughts about something that hasn't happened yet, so we can't take these thoughts to court. We need a different approach. Consider whatever you're worrying about, and run through the worst-case, best-case and most likely scenarios and attribute a percentage of likelihood to them. For example, say you've missed a mortgage payment.

- Imagine the worst-case scenario – e.g. house repossession and homelessness. One per cent likelihood, as you'd need to miss lots of payments in a row and take no action for that to happen.

- Imagine the best-case scenario – e.g. you get a sudden windfall and can pay immediately. Equally unlikely, odds-wise; perhaps one per cent?

- Consider the most likely scenario – e.g. you'll work on your budget and find ways to save and/or earn more and continue living in your home. About 99 per cent likely, as you're already thinking about the possibilities.

- Use reframing sentence structures based on what's most likely and what's possible to think from a more accurate perspective, such as:

  - "The most likely outcome is..."

  - "I can..."

- Create an action plan based on the most likely scenario. For example, phone and talk to your bank. They will likely understand and help you find a way to pay the arrears over time, without missing future payments.

Gaining perspective on the most likely eventuality often reveals the issue isn't as bad as you thought and gives you a solid plan of action to help you find a way through. By taking you from the most negative to the most absurdly positive solution, you can see how unrealistic your worst-case scenario thoughts are (it can also be fun coming up with ridiculously best-case scenarios) and you can practise more flexible, accurate and balanced thinking.

Now it's your turn:

I'm worried about: ....

....

The worst-case scenario would be if: ....

....

....

.... per cent likelihood

The best-case scenario would be if: ....

....

....

.... per cent likelihood

The most likely scenario is: ....

....

....

.... per cent likelihood

The truth is, worry won't make a problem better, but how you frame your thinking and respond to worrying thoughts can. We want helpful rather than unhelpful thoughts. The same is true of our feelings, which we'll explore on the following pages.

Part Two

FEEL: FEELINGS

Chapter Four

EXPRESSION

EDUCATED OUT OF EMOTION

"Hush now, don't cry." "Calm down!" "Don't be scared!" The messages are loud and clear – sad and mad are bad, happy and brave are good.

Consequently, our relationship with so-called negative emotions is adversarial. We've been conditioned to fight uncomfortable feelings, so we run from them, ignore them and judge them. Rather than being able to tolerate discomfort, we've been trained not to, so we are embarrassed by emotion, sorry for our sorrow and end up apologizing for being "too emotional". We don't like to impose our displays of emotion on others either; it makes us both feel awkward. And we've fostered the belief that expressing emotions – especially in public – will make us feel worse than we already do. What a shame given how it's when we are feeling down that we need support from others the most.

That's the purpose of emotion – to alert us and those around us that we have an urgent need. This negative-emotion averseness means we fail to permit ourselves to feel them, process them and even acknowledge them. We've got so bad at sad, we may not even be able to identify our more difficult emotions. This is nothing new though. It's generational. Grandparents who lived through a world war were told to "keep calm and carry on". Baby boomers and Generation X went further, prioritizing happiness and self-esteem, and demanding a positive mental attitude, sticking heads in the sand. The problem with self-esteem is it only serves you when you are doing well to encourage you to do even better. When you are making the inevitable mistakes that we all make in life, self-esteem deserts you, unlike self-compassion, which gives you a break even when you mess up – *especially* when you mess up.

We all struggle. We all feel sorrow. Emotional pain is a natural human response. Feeling bad is as normal as it is inevitable. It's how we're meant to feel in response to loss or disappointment.

FEELINGS AS FAILURE

So why do we pathologize sadness and other so-called negative emotions when it would serve us better to normalize them? It seems to stem from the Western obsession with the pursuit of happiness and success, which has framed sadness as failure and blames us for feeling such uncomfortable emotions. If you display your emotions publicly you are judged as being too sensitive or fragile. You might internalize the idea that there's something wrong with you if you feel unhappy or ashamed, as if you've somehow failed at life. Such pressure to be happy can lead those experiencing "normal" sadness to believe they are depressed. So how can you tell the difference? All emotions generally pass with time. Crying, venting, talking and journaling can offer relief. But, if feeling sad and helpless for longer than two weeks without relief, unable to function or laugh in between periods of sadness, this could be a sign of clinical depression. This is a mental illness rather than the normal human emotion of sadness, so keep track of your emotions, thoughts and physical experiences and consult your doctor.

The point is we've generally been conditioned to see pain as something to be fixed, sadness solved and discomfort avoided. Vulnerability has until recently been seen as a weakness. So, we push our feelings down, believing if we don't draw attention to them, then it can't hurt. But that does more harm than good.

SUPPRESSION VERSUS EXPRESSION

Denying our feelings and anaesthetizing our emotions doesn't work. In fact, choosing suppression over expression is more likely to backfire and make us feel worse. Feelings don't go away. They simmer under the surface until they either erupt or continue to fester and run the risk of turning ordinary unavoidable sadness into something more harmful as repression can lead to depression.

Avoidance of feelings can also lead to other life-diminishing behaviour, such as choosing not to risk trying in case we fail, or keeping our distance from others and avoiding closeness for fear of getting hurt, or numbing our pain and distracting ourselves by taking drugs, drinking alcohol, scrolling through social media or busying ourselves with work. Psychotherapist and grief counsellor Julia Samuel says, "It is not the pain of loss that damages individuals, but the things they do to *avoid* that pain." Here's why bottling up our emotions and choosing avoidance doesn't work and makes us feel worse:

- Trying not to feel something makes us feel it more. Harvard psychologist Daniel Wegner found those asked not to feel something sad were more likely to experience depressive or anxious thoughts.

- Unresolved emotions don't go away, they come back stronger, like unpaid bills. Psychologists call this amplification. If you shut the unpaid bill in a kitchen drawer and ignore it the problem doesn't go away. Pushing away your emotions is like ignoring those bills. You can't clear those debts. You just get more reminder letters to pay what you owe, with interest. The letters pile up and you accrue more debt than you started with. You need to deal with them. You need to pay. The same goes for emotions.

- Numbing our pain via drugs, alcohol, eating, shopping or other habits creates a new problem – addiction. They dilute the pain but also dilute our ability to cope with whatever it is we're running away from, which is sometimes ourselves. We'll still feel inadequate once we come down from our high, but now we're addicted.

- We become less practised and equipped to deal with those feelings the next time they inevitably crop up. The more we shield ourselves (and our children) from the inevitable adversities of life, and the more we try to fix or fight sadness rather than sitting with it, the less resilient we (and they) become. Enduring difficulty shows us our strengths and demonstrates what we're capable of coping with, which is often much more than we think.

- Busying ourselves to avoid pain leads to burnout. Keeping busy to keep going is a much-used coping mechanism. It comes from the fear that if we stop long enough to feel, uncomfortable feelings will rise up. But stored, ignored feelings fester and grow, so when burnout enforces stoppage, there's more to deal with.

- Numbing our pain means we numb our joy too, so we limit our life experience and only partially live. Conversely, when we stay open to feeling our sorrow, we stay open to feeling our delight.

- Ignoring what our feelings are trying to tell us prevents opportunities for growth or change. We stay stuck in the situations we are feeling down about. Conversely, when we listen to our emotions and heed their messages, we are more likely to make positive changes.

When we sit with discomfort and express our emotions, we process and move through them. Emotion is, after all, energy in motion (e-motion), so we need to let it move and speak (see page 134). The willpower needed to push down our feelings can be exhausting. Instead, we can use the energy for more meaningful pursuits.

What happens when we allow our feelings?

One study found that people who don't cry can experience more aggression, rage and disgust than those who do. The better we get at feeling our feelings, the better we cope. This is according to Northeastern University in Boston, USA, which found those who experience their emotions fully by working through them are less likely to get anxious or depressed or use unhealthy coping mechanisms. While research from the University of New South Wales in Sydney, Australia found the acceptance of temporary sadness increases our level of gratitude, our perseverance and improves both attention to detail and generosity.

Besides, we're designed to cry, not to hold our tears in. Tears have a purpose. Babies cry to get parents' attention and we are meant to cry to garner support. That's what tears are for – to release emotion and to request help – yet 74 per cent of us cry alone in the shower. Still, this is better than not crying at all. Crying reduces our cortisol levels and therefore decreases stress, while expressing sadness soothes us. We need to feel to heal. And, contrary to our conditioning, sad isn't bad. It's useful.

HELPFUL SIGNALS: THE GIFT OF FEELINGS

Feelings contain important messages, data that has something to show and teach us. Sorrow, anger, guilt and regret flag up when something needs our attention. They act as important warning signals that can prompt useful and positive change – be that in our own belief systems, responses and behaviour or to our environment, situation and circumstances.

Take shame, for example. When we feel shame, we focus on ourselves as a flawed person rather than on our flawed behaviour, which is both unhelpful and inaccurate. But shame can serve a purpose. When we feel shame in this way, it's signalling the need to change how we see ourselves, to work on our self-worth and change our beliefs. As such, the antidotes to shame are vulnerability, curiosity, empathy and self-compassion. When we lean into our vulnerability, share our shame and receive an empathetic response, that shame is reduced. And when we work on our own self-compassion and curiosity, we can question critical thoughts and replace them with more accurate ones.

Guilt, on the other hand, is behaviour-focused and rooted in blame rather than shame. For example, "I didn't make the team because I didn't practise much" (rather than "because I am bad at sport"), "I failed the test because I didn't revise enough" (rather than "because I am stupid"). Guilt comes from the observation that you did something bad or didn't do something good, so it's your fault/responsibility. Although unpleasant and uncomfortable, guilt can be helpful because it can drive positive change and behaviour, making us do something differently next time we're faced with a similar situation. The same is true of regret and disappointment (as explored on page 21).

Meanwhile, frustration and anger can signal our core values and what matters most to us. If I feel frustrated and angry because I've been accused of doing something I haven't done or because I see an inequality reported on the news, it signals my core values of fairness are being trodden on. I might then take positive action to make a change. So, what can we do to counter the cultural repression of emotion? To feel better, we need to feel our feelings better via awareness, acceptance and expression.

AWARENESS

We are not responsible for every experience, only for our responses to them. While we may not be able to control the past or all that will happen in the future, we can control our response to what has happened and what will come next.

STEP 13: Pay attention to your feelings

By paying attention to how we are feeling and creating space for curiosity, we can choose how best to respond.

● Recognize and label your feelings. Studies by the University of California revealed that simply labelling an emotion in a couple of words reduces the intensity of the feelings associated with it. This tool is used in mindfulness and by FBI hostage negotiators to calm situations down. Categorizing your feelings into types of emotion is a skill known as "emotion differentiation". The more we practise differentiating our emotions the better the mental health outcomes.

● Notice your bodily signals and connect them to emotions so you can regulate them. We often feel our emotions in our bodies first. The tight feeling in our chest when we're worried, the butterflies in our tummy when we're nervous or excited and the slump of our shoulders when we're sad. Interoception, a relatively new area of neuroscience and psychological study about our brain's perception of our bodily state, has found that noticing the "interoceptive signals" our bodies give us – and *connecting* those sensations with emotions – helps us self-regulate our emotions better and protect us from depression and anxiety.

The quicker we can connect our body's interoceptive signals to specific feelings, the quicker we can respond and self-regulate. Try the following:

● Practise noticing the physiological reactions your body makes in response to stimuli, such as bracing of breath, clenching of stomach and jaw, quickening of heartbeat, tension of muscles.

● Connect those interoceptive signals to emotions. Say, "I am feeling..."

- Regulate those emotions by choosing a strategy that promotes comfort within the body, such as slow-breathing techniques (see page 143), journaling (see page 67) or other interventions (see Part Three).

- Use metaphorical language to describe your feelings. What does this feeling feel like? For example, one of my best friends, Iva, keen to reply to my voice message with her own but wanting to feel more alert before doing so, said in a text message, "I feel like a droopy asparagus." I knew exactly what she meant. (Also, kudos to her for tuning in to her feelings so well and giving herself what she needed.) It can be hard to put feelings into words, so using a simile to explain that you feel as "grumpy as a wasp in a jar" can help define and take the sting out of such feelings (pun intended).

ACCEPTANCE

STEP 14: Accept all feelings and see them as helpful

We spend so much time regretting or ruminating on what's happened in the past, or worrying about what might happen in the future, but neither anxiety nor judgement can change either of those. In this way our memories and imaginations can become our own worst enemies and disable us. Things are rarely as bad as we imagine them to be and much is beyond our control. Accepting our imperfections and our past, the possibility that comes with uncertainty and all feelings across the full spectrum of human emotion, enables us.

REPRESS   EXPRESS/ALLOW   WALLOW

Negative emotions only have an adverse impact on health when they are *perceived* as bad and when we wallow in them rather than allow them. Accepting and allowing the inevitable curveballs of life rather than avoiding or wallowing is called "active acceptance" and it's imperative to finding emotional balance. We sometimes worry that if we spend time in sorrow, it will take over when the opposite is true. Giving sufficient space to sadness and focusing on awareness, acceptance and expression, we end up spending *less* time feeling sad overall because we have devoted time to *dealing* with it, and thus *healing* it. For instance, in relation to loss, rather than get over the loss or grow out of grief, with active acceptance we grow through it.

Yes, excessive negative *thinking* (rather than feelings) and pessimism can be detrimental to mental health, predictive of depression and can negatively impact our cognitive ability, making us less open to creative solutions. But, feeling bad about feeling bad can make us feel worse. And, as we've explored, so-called negative *feelings* that we've been conditioned to find uncomfortable are meaningful and valuable and should be viewed as such in order to flourish.

The steps that follow will help bring the balance back from the extremes of repression and wallowing to the more centred acceptance, allowing and expression of feelings.

STEP 15: Accept what you cannot change and change what you can

If we find ourselves ranting and complaining about what we have no control over, negativity can take over.

If we become aware that we are complaining more than appreciating, it's time to ask ourselves:

- Is this thing I'm complaining about within my control?
- How is it serving me to complain about it?
- Will it make a difference to the outcome?

According to meditation teacher and psychologist Tara Brach, "Radical acceptance means feeling sorrow and pain without resisting. It means feeling desire or dislike without judging ourselves or being driven to act on it." There may be no action required except expression and acceptance, but that is an action in itself.

Let it go flow chart

Take whatever's bothering you through this flow chart to decide whether to take action or let it go.

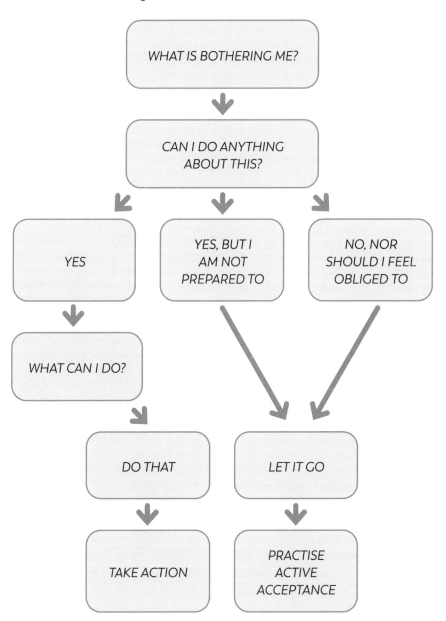

STEP 16: Cope with criticism

Our emotions are often evoked by other people. Humans hate criticism. As Aristotle said, "There is only one way to avoid criticism: do nothing, say nothing and be nothing." That said, if we reject constructive criticism we can hinder our own self-improvement. We can cope with criticism by:

- Deciding whether it's constructive or destructive – i.e. if you put your ego to one side and applied the suggestion to do something differently, might a better outcome be possible? If so, take it on board with thanks.

- If the criticism is not constructive, choose either to ignore it, remove yourself from the conversation or focus on curiosity over judgement and say, "how interesting they see it this way".

- Check in to ensure that inaccurate criticisms do not negatively impact your self-worth. There is no value in deciding to believe you are terrible at something when someone else's opinion is inaccurate. See page 49 for more on taking thoughts to court.

As I write in my book *You Are Enough*, the most important expectation to have about whether we are good enough is one that asks, "Am I being myself enough today?" As Polonius says in *Hamlet*, "To thine own self be true." So, are you being true to you? If you feel good about your daily choices and are living a life aligned with your own values, no matter what anyone else's opinion is, that's good enough. Your opinion of yourself is the most important of all.

EXPRESSION

STEP 17: Release your feelings

Crying is one way to reduce levels of cortisol, but did you know that getting angry can have the same impact? According to a study by Osnabrück University in Germany, participants who were made to feel angry experienced a significant decrease in cortisol afterwards. Anger can also be motivational, spurring us on to get stuff done. Because anger is associated with violence, we choose to avoid or suppress it, but – like all feelings – anger will only simmer and bubble over if not considered and released. Try the following:

- Address anger and frustration by first considering what is making you feel this way. An injustice? An unresolved frustration? Relentless poor treatment? It is likely a justifiable feeling, but it's worth double-checking the facts to ensure you're not boiling over when there may be a way to turn down the heat.

- Express anger by releasing it in a non-violent way. You could scream into a pillow, or in a parked car, for instance. A prolonged "aaaaaaargh" can be immensely therapeutic. Go for a run, cycle or a fast walk in the fresh air, or take some other form of exercise, such as boxing or kickboxing. Exercise reduces feelings of fear (a cortisol-raising culprit) and releases dopamine, easing stress and anger.

- Have a tantrum. Regular criers who don't suppress emotion can still hold on to trauma and frustration. Connected or transformational breathwork is a form of active meditation that can help release these. Lie down on a rug or yoga mat, with one hand on your belly and one on your heart. Breathe into your belly, into your heart, then exhale. And repeat: two breaths in, one breath out – belly, heart, exhale. Continue for 10–12 minutes. Then, make your hands into fists and pound the mat with your hands and stomp your feet.

STEP 18: Write it out

Pouring our hearts out through a pen on to a page can calm and boost us more than writing about something that isn't emotive. These findings were the results of a 40-year study by social psychologist James Pennebaker. Two groups of people were involved, with the first invited to write about their troubles for 20 minutes each day for three days; and the second asked to write for the same duration about ordinary everyday objects. The people in the first group were significantly happier and calmer than those in the second. Almost a year later those in the first group were having greater success at work, better relationships and were physically healthier. Give it a try. First focus on *what* and *how* you are feeling before you move on to the *why*. Just notice what/how you are feeling and note it down in your journal.

Journaling can help you come up with ideas, solutions and actions, or there may be no action once you've expressed feelings on the page. Whatever you record about your feelings will still have meaning. And the purpose of feelings is merely to be felt, experienced and expressed, so we can learn and grow.

Try using the following journal prompts. The first quickfire questions give you a chance to reflect on what might be troubling you in different ways:

What's bothering me most today is: ....

....

I'm feeling: ....

....

What's happening in my body: ....

....

What breaks my heart is: ....

....

If only: ....

....

I want to let go of: ....

....

It's time to make peace with: ....

....

Next, choose a specific issue and/or feeling to delve deeper into and uncover why you feel this way, and what can be learned and/or done to feel better.

What would happen if I applied acceptance, balance or compassion to how I'm feeling?

....

....

Are there any obvious lessons to learn from this challenge? (Instead of thinking, "Why is this happening to me?", consider what it is trying to teach you.)

....

....

Next consider *why* you are feeling this way. Has something happened or been said that steps on your values or triggers this response?

....

....

Write down what actions you could take to address the *why* behind the feeling. For example, talk to the person involved, get more sleep or exercise, consider another perspective (refer to Part Three for additional ideas).

....

....

STEP 19: Write a letter from your feelings

To get to the heart of the matter and uncover what your feelings are trying to tell you, give your emotions a seat at the table; metaphorically hand them the mic. Let them explain *why* they are feeling this way. Over to you, feelings...

- Your fear might say, "I feel scared because I don't want you to get hurt."

- Sadness might say, "I feel sad because you didn't get invited to that party."

- Frustration might say, "I feel frustrated because of how unfair it is that you give so much, but are still spoken to in that way."

- Jealousy might say, "I'm worried you might lose them and I don't want that to happen."

The trick on your journey through life is to give those emotions (which were previously considered as "negative") a seat in the car, but don't let them drive. Remember, ignoring them backfires. Take fear, for example. Ignoring fear completely and taking a risk without consideration could be dangerous, because fear is there for a reason – to protect us. However, handing full control over to fear means we stop doing potentially life-enhancing stuff that fear is afraid of. That's when fear becomes boring, as it prevents us from doing beneficial things that would show us what we're capable of and boost our confidence. The right balance is to listen to fear and find out what's behind it. Try writing a letter to yourself from your fear.

What does fear have to say? By befriending fear we get to "feel the fear and do it anyway" – we get to move forward.

STEP 20: Talk it out

- Reach out to friends. Sometimes people don't want to bring up a loss you've experienced for fear of reminding you of it, especially if you're trying to put on a brave face and seem "fine". Equally those who've experienced loss can be reluctant to share how they're feeling, for fear of bringing others down. This form of suppression serves nobody. The best approach is openness – for the person who has experienced loss, the worst has already happened, so you can't make them feel worse by inviting them to share their feelings. For their friend, the loss can feel like an elephant in the room, so it's a relief to be able to talk about it freely and step into that supportive role. Reaching out is always better than retreating. If you notice retreating is your go-to coping mechanism during tough times, push yourself to pick up the phone, send a text and say, "I'm feeling low, any chance of a chat?" Your friends want you to ask for help, just as you want them to ask if they need you. Always remember, you are never a burden to your friends, because friends are there to offer connection and support. Talking about your feelings can be powerful enough to reduce their impact and make you feel better.

- Practise empathy. Rather than tell people to "stay positive" or "keep their chin up", invite them to tell you how they're feeling and let them know you're there for them. Let them know you understand what they're experiencing is difficult, validate the hardship rather than minimize it and ask how you might be able to help support them.

- Book a talking therapy session. For those who can't get past the need to protect the listener from their woes, therapists are there for you to talk to about anything without having to worry about how it will make them feel. It is their job to help you uncover and make sense of the true narratives behind your story and express your emotions.

- Practise vulnerability. Brené Brown found that vulnerability is the antidote to shame and, rather than being a weakness, recasts vulnerability as a strength. In my book, *Navigating Loneliness*, I talk about how vulnerability bolsters connection with others. When we share our vulnerability other people are more likely to relate and share their vulnerability too. Leadership studies have found those who open up to their staff cultivate deeper trust and connections and retain staff loyalty. Vulnerability connects people.

STEP 21: Use music to express emotions

Music is a supportive companion. It has the power to soothe feelings, reduce stress and calm us down. It can also fire us up and get us bouncing around to release nervous energy – or even induce tears if we need to express and release our emotions by crying them out. Our heightened emotional response to music can be due to the pace or lyrics, or the bittersweet memory associated with it. Given that musicians often write about their own emotional experiences, listening to music can also foster a sense of belonging, helping us feel like we're not alone in feeling the way we do. Classical music has been shown to speed up and enhance physical recovery, while music therapy – both listening to and making it – has been shown to reduce psychological stress, depression and anxiety. See page 79.

Given that music provides the soundtrack to our lives, we can tap into its power to be the DJ of our own emotional disco. Create a range of playlists for when you are feeling a certain way. (This will also help you define and label your emotions.) You could try:

- A happy playlist.
- An angry playlist.
- A heartbreak playlist.

As well as listening to music, try making some too.

- Learn to play an instrument. A Spotify study revealed 89 per cent of UK adults who regularly play an instrument feel relaxed, satisfied and peaceful. You can play your instrument when feeling a certain way to express your emotions.

- Join a drumming circle. Drumming can feel like a primeval connection to our heartbeat (and a way to release feelings), while drum vibrations can be hypnotic. Pay attention to the tempo, volume and rhythm of your drumming and get lost in the beat.

- Sing to release dopamine and express feelings, whether in the shower, car or doing housework, or grow the Relationships and Accomplishment branches of well-being by joining a choir.

STEP 22: Try art therapy

There are various ways to use art to express your feelings and, as Dodie Smith's Cassandra Mortmain says in *I Capture the Castle*, "Art can make sad things beautiful." Try these:

- Draw or paint your feelings onto paper or canvas. Close your eyes first and tune in to your body. How do you feel? If that feeling had a colour, shape and texture, what would it be? Would that feeling be heavy or light, hot or cold, flexible or rigid? Would the lines be straight, squiggly, zig-zag or jagged? Use those colours, textures and patterns in your art. For a mixed-media effect, tear relevant words out of magazines and glue to your art piece.

- Write a stream of consciousness of words onto the page about how you are feeling. I learned this technique from my good friend Tanis Frame, who runs a Decide to Thrive immersion programme on ways to thrive in our lives. You can write anything because you'll cover it up with paint. Now repeat the previous exercise and paint over the words with resonant colours, lines and so on.

- Draw a heart and fill it with a range of patterns and colours that represent how you are feeling right now in this moment.

- Draw a valley at one end of a piece of paper and a mountain at the other end. Think about a time when you felt at your lowest and draw or paint whatever comes to mind in the valley section of your piece. Now think about a time when you felt at your happiest and draw or paint whatever comes to mind in the mountain section. You could add to the picture with a flowing river or bridges and other metaphorical images.

- Colour in pages filled with designs and words that resonate with how you're feeling. My own *Flourish Colouring Book* features affirmations and questions to colour in.

STEP 23: Take action

For situations we have some control over, our feelings can serve as a call to action – to do something that will empower us and reduce the feeling. For example:

- Try exposure therapy and in small doses do something that scares you; gradually increase the time you spend doing it until you are no longer scared of it.

- Forgive. Those who forgive experience fewer negative emotions than those who do not. They feel better rather than bitter, because in forgiving they regain control.

- Speak out and become an activist about the issues you care deeply about.

- Donate to charities and/or volunteer your time or expertise to help those causes that matter most to you.

- Find purposeful work that makes a difference in the care/education/social sector.

Taking action feels good, whether through actively expressing our feelings, doing something differently with the benefit of hindsight, or responding to our own personal call to action. Action enables us to move forward, to grow and, ultimately, to flourish. So, about that...

Part Three

DO:
ACTIONS

Chapter Five
P IS FOR POSITIVE EMOTION

Positive psychology interventions are a proven practical way to build the six branches of well-being (PERMA-V), which are:

P – Positive emotion
E – Engagement
R – Relationships
M – Meaning
A – Accomplishment
V – Vitality

> *Positive emotion does much more than just feel pleasant; it is a neon sign that growth is under way, that psychological capital is accumulating.*

Martin Seligman

During the 1970s, psychologists studying emotions focused on "hedonic capacity", our ability to feel pleasure. Since then, the focus has shifted toward "affectivity", the extent to which an individual experiences positive/negative moods. That extent is measured by what researchers call "positive affect" and "negative affect", and we now know we can improve our positive affectivity (our propensity to experience positive emotions) via what we do – our daily actions.

Why positive emotions are important

In the late 1990s, researcher and psychologist Barbara Fredrickson wanted to find out why we evolved to have positive emotions. After all, negative emotions had served an evolutionary purpose of survival – to engage our fight-or-flight response. So, what purpose did positive emotions serve? She carried out multiple lab-controlled experiments, which provided some fascinating findings about positivity.

It turns out that positive emotion interventions (like those included throughout this chapter) are worthwhile investments because those with high positive affectivity tend to perform, communicate and express themselves better, have healthier relationships, healthier hearts and build capacity to heal faster. So, positive emotions enable the optimal human functioning of flourishing.

Fredrickson discovered that experiencing positive emotions also helps us bounce back sooner after experiencing the inevitable setbacks of life, and think with greater clarity so we can use this improved brain function to solve whatever problems we've been stressing out about. The more we cumulatively deposit into our positive emotions "bank account" over time, the more we build, not just psychological strengths, but our intellectual, physical and social resources too, such as our openness to learning and problem-solving capabilities, our cardiovascular health, our coordination and ability to create and maintain relationships. Ultimately, positive emotions are a vital tool in helping us navigate the twists and turns of everyday life. Here's why:

Positive emotions...

- Counter our inbuilt evolutionary negativity bias, enabling us to bring the balance back and swing the pendulum toward flourishing.

- Broaden our thought–action cognitive and behavioural repertoires, i.e. our ability to think clearly to influence our behaviour. Fredrickson's "broaden-and-build" theory shows that we think more clearly and creatively as our ability to think outside the box broadens when experiencing positive emotions. Conversely negative emotions narrow and restrict our cognitive capacity rather than expand it.

- Build and bank our resilience, optimism and other psychological resources that we can store in our "positivity reserves" and draw upon during times of need. The more these strengths develop, the better we feel, building our personal resources in an upward spiral.

When we're feeling down, we can increase positive emotions by participating in certain activities to lift us up and dilute negative emotions. (Fredrickson found stressed-out bodies were able to return to normal physiological functioning much sooner after experiencing positive emotions than control groups.) Or by weaving such activities into days when we're feeling fine, to sustain our good mood and optimize our wellness. Either way it's possible to facilitate flourishing and be at our best by doing stuff that lifts us up.

STEP 24: Make a flourish list

Write a list of seven things you can do quickly and easily to nourish rather than numb you and cultivate any of the following emotions: joy, gratitude, serenity, interest, hope, pride, amusement, inspiration, awe and love.

This is what to do if you need a quick boost of positive emotions, such as phoning a friend, connecting with nature, or dancing to some upbeat music. Here's my flourish list:

1. Go outside and birdwatch. Listen to birdsong.

2. Hug (daughter, dogs or tree).

3. Make a nice cup of tea. Sip slowly.

4. Read a chapter of a book. Savour each word and the softness of the page.

5. Stand barefoot on grass and SLUB (Stop. Look Up. Breathe).

6. Raise your mental and physical energy levels and SAD (Stop. And. Dance).

7. Go for a woodland walk or wild swim.

Your turn. My flourish list:

1. ....

2. ....

3. ....

4. ....

5. ....

6. ....

7. ....

Rewrite this on a card and pop in your wallet or on a wall, or take a photo to store on your phone so you see it often and use it regularly.

STEP 25: Get creative with (or for) friends

We know that art can be a useful tool for expressing emotions (see page 72), but it's also a valuable well-being boosting activity in its own right. A New Zealand diary study of 650 young adults, which measured the correlation between creativity and well-being, discovered small acts of daily creativity boosted a general sense of well-being the following day. Participants reported feeling happier and more energized, with a positive mood, during and after creative activity. And, if you can get creative with (or for) friends, you can amplify the effect. You could try the following:

- Go on regular meaningful art dates with friends. This can grow multiple branches of well-being. For example, when Joanna, a childhood friend of mine, was facing health struggles, a group of us gathered at our local art hub to paint pottery or do decoupage, making keepsakes for loved ones and giving her something to look forward to. We'd burst with positive emotion after each laughter-filled session (I'll never forget her laugh) and lose track of time, so engaged were we in the activity. We grew our supportive relationships branch and felt accomplished when we completed our meaningful creations. (Five out of six PERMA-V boxes ticked!)

- Paint thank-you cards for friends. An abundance of positive emotions will emerge from a) the creative process itself, b) the feelings of gratitude captured and c) the act of giving.

STEP 26: Enjoy a sonic tonic

Sound-bathing has become increasingly popular in recent times. Immersion in the meditative sound of gongs, crystal and singing bowls originated in Tibet thousands of years ago. The sound waves slow our pulse, destress our minds, reduce blood pressure and soothe our nervous system more than meditation alone, offering deep relaxation.

As I touched on previously, music, too, is medicine for our modern-day maladies. As the field of neuro-musicology reveals, music can have significant impact on our brains. Live music has been shown to reduce stress hormones like cortisol, while calming tunes like "Weightless" by Marconi Union – specifically designed to slow the heart rate, reduce blood pressure and lower cortisol levels – has been proven to reduce anxiety by 65 per cent.

STEP 27: Get nourished by novels and non-fiction

Mindlab International Research revealed that reading reduces stress by 67 per cent. In 2013, doctors drew up a list of 27 mood-boosting books, distributed as part of a "Books on Prescription" scheme, supported by the UK Department for Health. Visit cherylrickman.co.uk for this list.

Brain scans of readers have shown the act of reading positively stimulates our neural pathways as we "mentally rehearse" the sensory delights of a story as it unfolds. Our empathy levels rise when we read too, which helps us better connect with people in the real world. Escaping into someone else's narrative can be consoling and reassuring, providing an opportunity to relate to and feel kinship with others, to feel understood in a world that misunderstands; to feel like we are not alone in our experiences when we read about others who've faced similar challenges. Stories of struggles and triumphs inspire us, and explore the full spectrum of human experience across time periods, country borders, cultures and perspectives and remind us of the power of the human spirit. Why not try the following:

- Amplify the power of reading by creating a cosy book nook, a serene space in which to curl up and retreat when alone.

- Find opportunities to be read to and add another level of nurturing comfort. Set up a reading club, where friends gather monthly to read their favourite passages from books to each other.

- Create a seasonal ritual of taking books you've read to the local charity shop and replacing them with new ones. You'll gain the expectant delight of having new reading material, plus the added benefit of giver's glow – a positive emotion infusion.

Cultivate an attitude of gratitude

We are all dreaming of some magical rose garden over the horizon – instead of enjoying the roses blooming outside our windows today.

Dale Carnegie

If it could be bottled, gratitude would be a wonder drug. We can literally change our brains and bodies for the better by being grateful. Yet we get so caught up in our future yearnings that we forget to count our current blessings; we miss the *presents* in our present. There are a few reasons why this is so:

🍃 The overt busyness of modern life can take our focus away from enjoying the "now".

🍃 We tend to take life for granted. Our six-year-old selves don't cherish the boundless energy we have or the time we get to spend playing. And if only we'd appreciated our 21-year-old selves more.

🍃 Our evolutionary survival wiring makes us remember and react more strongly to negative stimuli than to positive stimuli.

Consequently, we need to train our brains to appreciate more. Gratitude has been called "a natural antidepressant" because of the way it biologically affects the brain and boosts dopamine and oxytocin. According to neuroscience studies on brain activity and morphology carried out by the Universities of California and Miami, when people intentionally practise gratitude the flow of feel-good neurochemicals in the brain multiplies and the neural structure is literally re-sculpted. As such, by devoting more attention to appreciation, we can develop happier brains. Additionally, according to the HeartMath Institute, our brains work better following a gratitude practice. And those who habitually feel and articulate gratitude perform better, sleep better and see health and relationship improvements.

Gratitude can help us heal better too. Of 186 people with heart conditions, a University of California study found the more grateful participants were also the happiest and healthiest. After undertaking a gratitude practice for two months, blood tests revealed lower inflammation and improved heart health.

Of course, humans being humans, when we're feeling low, we might feel guilty about our lack of gratitude for what we have. In those instances, give yourself permission to be human, remind yourself that longing is part of the human condition even when we have what we want, then do something to lift yourself up (revisit your flourish list on page 78) and be grateful that you did. It's not always easy to find the good, but there's always *something* to be grateful for – from fresh water and good health to the doting attention of a pet.

STEP 28: Find the good – seek and notice what to be grateful for

🍃 Replace "I've got to" with "I get to". Instead of thinking, "I've got to stop this task to collect the kids," think, "I get to spend time in the car with the kids, which is often the best time to talk to them." Try it here:

I've got to ....

I get to ....

I've got to ....

I get to ....

I've got to ....

I get to ....

🍃 Savour feelings of gratitude for at least 10 seconds to install the positive experience in your memory bank and amplify the impact of appreciation. The longer we spend savouring the good, the more our neurons fire and wire together.

🍃 Attach your gratitude practice to another activity. For example, studies show that people who took savouring gratitude walks each day for one week significantly boosted their well-being levels compared with those who walked as normal.

- Plan experiences you'll be grateful for in future and reminisce on past events you're thankful to have enjoyed. By anticipating an event, enjoying it as it happens, then recalling that fond memory by looking back at photographs, we can feel grateful for a single moment three times.

STEP 29: Express, record and reminisce on what you are grateful for

- Record what went well in a gratitude journal. Jot down three good things that went well today and every day for the next two weeks. Also note why those things went well. This will help you to focus on the actual sources of goodness, and on how each good thing made you feel. More than 500 participants in Martin Seligman's online "Authentic Happiness" study (2005) who regularly recorded three good things repoted that their moods improved, and they felt happier and less depressed, for up to six months after they began the intervention. For example, you could write the following:

Thank you. I am grateful for the following three things that went well today.

1. ....

Why did this go well?...

2. ....

Why did this go well?...

3. ....

Why did this go well?...

- Organize a gratitude visit. According to Seligman, this is one of the most effective happiness-boosting exercises. Consider who has made a genuine difference to your life – someone you've never properly thanked. If they live or work close enough to visit, write a letter thanking them in detail for the specific positive impact they've had on your life. Arrange to visit them, without revealing your intention, and when you visit, read out your letter to them.

- Imagine the absence of something you feel grateful for. Imagining something hasn't happened heightens how thankful we feel that it did. This is called mental-subtraction and participants in this intervention reportedly felt deeper gratitude than those who reminisced on past happy events without picturing an absence.

- Write a gratitude reminder to your "meh" self from your "yay" self – a note on your phone or in a notebook that lists all the good stuff in your life. Read these reminders whenever low mood makes you forget what is good.

- Keep a list of delight on your phone that you add to any time you find delight in something ordinary – from the softness of a book page and the sound of birdsong, to the scent of rain on dry earth.

- See things through the eyes of someone who desperately wants what you have. For example, your pet Labrador through the eyes of your child self who longed for a dog; your running water through the eyes of someone less fortunate.

The branches of well-being we'll explore across the next few chapters will also generate positive emotions. For example, engagement interventions will likely inspire interest, inspiration and amusement, as will meaning interventions. While relationships interventions may bring about love, inspiration, amusement, hope, pride and interest, accomplishment interventions could generate pride, joy, hope, gratitude and inspiration, and vitality interventions might evoke pride and gratitude. That's the beauty of flourishing – the growth of one branch leads to the growth of another.

Chapter Six

E IS FOR ENGAGEMENT

Life is rich with experiences, but how might you enjoy "optimal experience"? That's what Engagement is all about. This branch of well-being was added to the PERMA-V mnemonic when Mihaly Csikszentmihalyi, a Hungarian psychologist with a penchant for mountain climbing, joined Martin Seligman and Ray Fowler to come up with the core foundations of positive psychology. This sense of sustained involvement where the engaging activity itself is its own reward, where nothing else matters except the activity engaged in, is known as "flow" or "optimal experience". Flow is a deeply involved state and a heightened level of engagement; where we are so absorbed in what we are doing that time seems to stand still and we lose track of time – for example, when musicians feel they "become one with the music", or when athletes lose all sense of the crowd being there.

Csikszentmihalyi first discovered flow himself while climbing mountains. Later, while researching his book, he asked people what they were thinking when they were in flow and they repeatedly replied, "nothing".

What is flow?

Our regular state of mind – where we continually interrupt our activities and thoughts with questions, judgements and concerns – is called "entropy". "Should I be doing this now?", "I can't believe he/she said that", "I wonder how so-and-so is?", "I must remember to put the rubbish/dog/ recycling out", and so on.

Conversely, flow offers freedom from entropy as it allows everyday concerns and thoughts to momentarily leave us. So, flow is the ultimate way to enjoy the journey and be fully present in the moment. It literally frees us from regrets about the past or fears about the future; and, as Csikszentmihalyi says in *Flow: The Psychology of Optimal Experience*, frees us from "being held hostage to a hypothetical future gain".

STEP 30: Find activities that fit flow criteria

Given that such optimal experience is not our natural state, flow is something we need to make happen ourselves, by embarking on activities that engage us and fit certain criteria. Engagement in flow activities is about mastery, participation and control. In his book, *Flow: The Psychology of Happiness,* Csikszentmihalyi outlines the criteria that activities require to generate this state. These activities must allow us to:

- Complete them due to our adequate skills.
- Concentrate on them.
- Exercise control over them.
- Set clear goals around them.
- Gain immediate feedback regarding how well we're doing.
- Lose self-consciousness.
- Forget about everyday worries.
- Lose track of time, so an hour feels like a matter of minutes or vice versa.

STEP 31: Make the mundane engaging – gamify the everyday

Engaging activities should be sufficiently challenging, but not so difficult that you lose enjoyment or so easy that you get bored. Sporting activities tick this box – tennis or football, dancing or climbing. Artistic activities and games with the right level of challenge tick this box too, such as painting or playing chess. We should absolutely schedule such activities into our lives, but even seemingly mundane tasks can be adapted by implementing the criteria of flow. For example, in focusing your attention on mowing the lawn, setting a time limit to mow a certain area and scoring points for accuracy, the act of lawn-mowing can become engaging and more enjoyable. Similarly, tiresome work tasks can be transformed into optimal experiences. Indeed, Csikszentmihalyi discovered that people reported more flow situations at work than they did in leisure activities. Think of ways you could turn mundane activities into flow experiences and turn tasks into a game. You just need clear rules, immediate feedback and time pressure.

STEP 32: Make time for fun

Of course, engagement isn't only about flow; it's also about fun. When we're having fun, we're fully engaged in the moment. Here are a few ways to bring more engagement and fun into your days:

- Play more. Write down what you loved doing when you were ten years old and tap into the enthusiasm you had as a child. For example, rolling down grassy hills and jumping through sprinklers with friends, roller-skating, hula-hooping, den-building, tree-climbing or doing dance routines. How might you bring some of those playful activities back into your life?

- Adventure. Step boldly outside of your comfort zone. Nudge yourself toward the unfamiliar and do something challenging you wouldn't ordinarily do. (Note: adventure is another activity that grows all six of the branches of well-being and often proves you can do more than you thought you could.)

- Be spontaneous. Place the following pick 'n' mix of engaging activities into a jar and pick one each weekend.

Fun activities pick 'n' mix

- Learn to juggle
- Fly a kite
- Build a den
- Climb a tree
- Climb a mountain
- Choreograph a dance routine
- Put on a show
- Go sailing
- Go kayaking
- Go paddleboarding
- Go fishing
- Go orienteering
- Go bowling
- Go ice-skating
- Bounce on a trampoline
- Play chess
- Play a board game
- Play a ball game
- Create a vision board
- Make birthday cards
- Ride on horseback
- Learn something new
- Host a hula-hooping comp
- Join a choir
- Build a tower from blocks
- Plant a hanging basket

Chapter Seven

R IS FOR RELATIONSHIPS

*Of all the things that wisdom provides
to help one live one's entire life in happiness,
the greatest so far is friendship.*

Epicurus

Relationships, eh? They can be tricky given how many variables of communication we have and how complex we are. Everything we say, our tone of voice, facial expression, body language is interpreted and responded to based on other people's personal values, beliefs and mood. No wonder the potential for misunderstanding and conflict is high. Relationships make us feel things deeply too. They make us feel love and hope and gratitude, but also anger, frustration and disappointment. Other people have the power to lift us up or bring us down. So, when it comes to well-being, those people are fundamental to flourishing.

Why other people matter

Good company is good for us. Strong, supportive relationships mitigate stress and are an essential source of satisfaction, keeping us happier and healthier. An array of data confirms this, including an 84-year-old Harvard study of adult development, which began in 1939 and continues today. Specifically, brains stay healthier, nervous systems relax and emotional pain is reduced when we have someone in our life we can rely on. As intrinsically tribal beings by nature, connection with other humans gives us a sense of love and belonging, which – once our basic safety and physiological needs have been fulfilled – are the next most vital. Knowing we can both give and receive support enables us to not only survive, but also thrive. Good relationships create a comforting sense of trust, valuable in a world that can feel uncertain and uncomfortable.

Human connection has a positive reassuring impact, not just on our minds but our physiology too. Oxytocin is a neurotransmitter and hormone produced when we interact with others. This feel-good chemical calms us down, lifts us up and opens us up to further connection, making us more willing to be friendly. This, in turn, boosts oxytocin production in the person we're being friendly toward, triggering mutual connection and care. In this way oxytocin is part of our "calm and connect" response (as opposed to our "fight-or-flight" response). So, when oxytocin is produced it moderates the reactivity of the amygdala (our emotional brain), enabling us to think more clearly and become open to connection opportunities.

Brain coupling

When we establish eye contact with someone or hear their voice, we share a real-time sensory connection that can induce a shared positive emotion. This, says Barbara Fredrickson, "unfurl[s] across two brains and bodies at the same time". During these micro-moments of synchronized positive connection, a chain reaction occurs. "There is one state and one emotion," says Fredrickson. "A miniature version of a mind meld." In this way, sharing a positive story and listening to it becomes a single, shared process performed by two brains. The same parts of our brains are activated in parallel with each other. This is known as "brain-coupling" and causes us to literally be on the same wavelength at that moment of connection. Brain-coupling opens us up to the other person, heightening our inclination to care about them. This positivity resonance is amplified back and forth between us, increasing how willing we are to care about each other's well-being. Deep connection that fosters caring: how beautiful is that? This explains why connection via text or email doesn't have quite the same positivity resonance effect, because the connection must be face to face or, at the very least, via the telephone or video-call.

Everyone needs to feel seen and heard. But we don't need a party bus full of friends to feel this way. To nurture and develop our supportive relationships and grow this branch of well-being, here's what we *do* need:

- Circles of connection with the right people.
- Positive communication.
- Sufficient time to connect.

So, let's tackle these step by step.

Circles of connection with the right people

Inner circle: Having a close connection with one or two people buffers against mental illness and bolsters mental wellness. According to loneliness expert, Professor John Cacioppo, if we have at least one close friendship, plus a relationship network of five or more key "confidant(e)s", we're less likely to be lonely.

Middle circle: Experts call this network our relational "sympathy group", which might include people who make us laugh, whom we feel we can talk to, but we likely don't connect on a deeper level. We can stave off loneliness with five close friends and 15 in our middle circle.

Outer circle: Being part of this wider group of acquaintances gives us our sense of social identity and makes us feel like we belong somewhere. We might talk about the weather and less meaningful topics, but it can still be comforting to have a little interaction with this outer circle.

STEP 33: Consider your circles

Your "social account" is the level of good-quality healthy connections you currently have and, given the impact on well-being, it's worth periodically checking your balance. The more you invest in the right relationships for you, the healthier your social account balance will be.

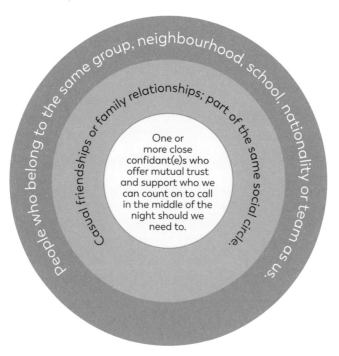

One or more close confidant(e)s who offer mutual trust and support who we can count on to call in the middle of the night should we need to.

Casual friendships or family relationships; part of the same social circle.

people who belong to the same group, neighbourhood, school, nationality or team as us.

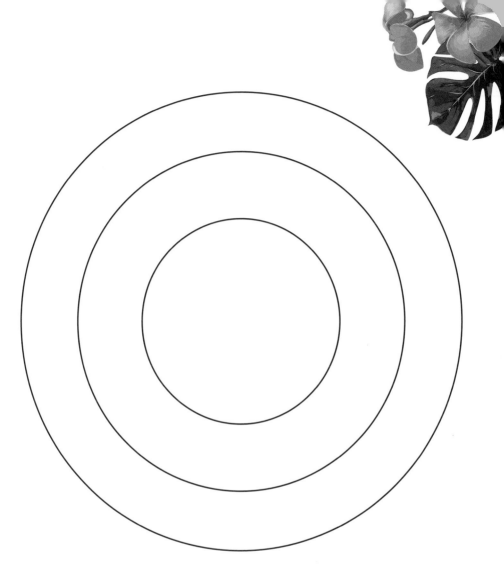

Write the names of one to seven people you consider to be in your inner circle, one to 15 people in your middle circle and anyone in your outer circle above. You might not consider those in your outer circle as important, but completing this exercise could remind you that a wave from a neighbour matters more than you'd realized. Different friends offer different "nutrients". Surround yourself with people who nourish you, then nurture these nutrient-rich relationships by investing time in them.

Rate your relationships

Next to each name in your inner and middle circles, write down what each relationship gives you. For example: encouragement, laughter, energy, understanding, interest, comfort, fun, inspiration, reassurance, resonance, a container for parental concerns, good advice. Get specific.

Add other reasons why you feel connected to this person. For example, they might have been through a similar experience, have children of similar ages or show an interest in your work. They might be great at giving advice or simply listening and encouraging. They might be good at distracting you by making you laugh, or perhaps you feel you can be your true self in their company.

STEP 34: Nurture and nourish your inner circle connections

What can you do to nurture your most nourishing nutrient-rich relationships further? For example, organize a brunch date/takeaway evening on the last Saturday of each month, visit a garden centre with them at the beginning of each new season or send something meaningful in the post. Write a list here:

....

....

....

....

....

You could also try doing the following:

- Schedule these into your flourish planner on pages 148–9.

- Practise a loving-kindness meditation regularly. Loving-kindness is the desire for people, including yourself, to be happy and well. It's an opening of the heart. This has been proven to boost positivity resonance (see page 91), along with cognitive, social and psychological resources. Find a loving-kindness meditation audio online.

Positive communication

Relationships are about relating. How we talk, listen and respond makes a difference to how well we relate and how mutually supportive our relationships are.

STEP 35: Practise talking well

Talking helps us feel better. When we talk about a problem it hasn't just been shared but aired – and that helps. Articulating a situation opens the door to express how we feel about it – "Better out than in," as my mum used to say. Talking things through makes you feel lighter, supported and, often, more hopeful when you get things out of your head. And, while it's good to talk in real time, even leaving a voicemail or a voice note – so your friend can respond when they have time – can be cathartic. What we talk about and how we say it also has an impact on how we make each other feel.

Non-violent communication (NVC)

It's easy to become judgemental or defensive during communication. In the 1960s, through his work as a civil-rights activist and mediator, clinical psychologist Marshall Rosenberg developed a form of communication called "non-violent communication" (NVC) based on compassion and empathy.

NVC recognizes that we share the same universal human needs – to be heard and respected – and that we all have capacity for compassion. Indeed, compassion is a deeply wired human instinct that aided our species' survival. When we see somebody in distress, our vagus nerve activates and directs us toward compassion.

So, NVC is a process of observing without judgement, expressing feelings and needs, and then requesting how those needs might be attended to. It involves clearly expressing facts without demanding, blaming or criticizing. But it takes practice. When we get to express ourselves honestly in a non-confrontational and non-defensive manner, relationships flourish. For instance, instead of, "You kept me up all night with the TV blaring. You're so selfish!" an NVC option would be: "I noticed the TV was on loudly when I woke up in the early hours. It made me feel annoyed because I need my sleep. I'd like it if the volume on the TV could be turned down earlier."

Write down what you might say to someone about something that is bugging you.

....

....

....

Now write down an NVC way of communicating your:

Observation: ....

Feeling: ....

Need: ....

Request: ....

Other techniques that minimize conflict:

- Use "I" rather than "you" messages to avoid defensiveness. For example, rather than, "You're being unreasonable! You're confusing me!"; you could say, "I'm upset because I don't understand and it sounds like it might be unreasonable, can you explain?" It's far better to request clarification than invite a fight.

- Avoid generalizations, absolutes and judgement, which can result in confrontation with those who disagree and disable discussion.

- Be open to dropping contentious subjects, agreeing to disagree, and setting boundaries to avoid discussing topics that create friction and pollute relationships unnecessarily. Some people love political debate; others avoid it. Understand and honour people's boundaries.

STEP 36: Practise listening well

Good relationships are about give and take, so, in the interest of balance and the benefits of offering support as well as receiving it, listening well is critical. Sometimes when someone is talking it can be easy to get stuck on a point of disagreement, but this can prevent what follows from being heard. Or we might start working out our response, such as an experience of our own that relates to what the person has just said, which also gets in the way of listening fully. There are certain rules that good listeners abide by. When listening actively:

- Do maintain eye contact and nod to demonstrate attention.
- Don't look at something or someone else or (even worse) at your phone.
- Do listen without judgement if possible. You can ponder about what has been said and form opinions later but, in the moment, just hear what the person has to say.
- Don't interrupt.

STEP 37: Practise responding well

Good communication to foster supportive relationships isn't just about how well we listen, it's about how well we respond, both to what people are struggling with and what they are celebrating.

Responding to good news

As well as encouraging people to talk about experiences that lift them up and listening actively with interest, how we respond to each other's good news is, according to research by the University of California, more indicative of a strong relationship than how we respond to bad news! There are four types of response:

1. Passive constructive. The most common response involves minimal celebration or support and lacks enthusiasm or interest, such as "Oh, that's nice..."

2. Passive destructive shifts the focus away from the speaker's good news on to your own. "Oh really? Well, I've had a promotion too. It was amazing because..."

3. Active destructive response removes the joy from the news by diluting it. For example, "A promotion? But you'll be so tired with longer hours. And what about childcare?"

4. Active constructive response. The best (and only reasonable) way to respond to good news. This helps the speaker relive their positive experience so they can capitalize on the good event while you share

in the celebration. This involves enthusiastic support with eye contact and plenty of smiles while they share their news, followed by questions that draw out more details, helping the speaker to savour what they're celebrating. For example, "That's amazing! So how did you feel when they...?" "Ooh, and what happened next...?"

Responding to struggles

The "support" in "supportive" can look different to what we might expect. Not everyone sharing their problems wants you to come up with solutions – they may just want to vent and could feel that taking advice makes them feel inadequate. If, like me, you are a rescuer/fixer and people pleaser, it can be difficult not to rush to advise. Furthermore, rejected "rescues" can leave us dejected as we were only trying to help. Caring deeply is a superpower and should not be discouraged, yet it's important to understand what the person struggling actually wants support-wise.

Sometimes the best way to respond is to simply hold space and listen, without judgement. The person sharing might benefit more from figuring it out themselves after talking about it. What if we trust that this person has their own answers? How might this relationship shift? Other people's happiness is not always our responsibility. What if, rather than see this as rejection, we saw it as an opportunity to put down something heavy that isn't ours to carry – i.e. the weight of everyone else's happiness?

Balance hearing with helping

If you are a rescuer/fixer by default:

- Ask whether the person talking would prefer you to just listen or whether they'd be interested in your input too.

- Listen attentively either way. Then, when you're alone you could jot down potential solutions, observations or ideas ready to share (but only if you're invited to do so later).

- Ask questions that might help the other person come up with their own answers and solutions.

If you struggle to receive support:

- Ask yourself whether the problem you are sharing might benefit from external input. Caring people love to offer advice and a different perspective could shift yours or provide a valid answer.

- Know that receiving advice or help does not make you inadequate. We are tribal creatures who are meant to help each other. By permitting others to help, you are making them feel good (read more about helpers' high on page 113) and potentially resolving a struggle or releasing a challenge.

STEP 38: Balance nourishing your soul with playing your roles

We often define ourselves by who we support and love, by our relationships (e.g. parent, sibling, partner, friend, daughter/son).

Jot down who you support and what you do to support them:

....

....

....

....

Who supports you and how?

....

....

Is this well-balanced? Do you have sufficient support? If not, what might you do to change that?

....

....

....

Time to connect

Busyness gets in the way of supportive relationships. But there are ways we can optimize our connection time.

STEP 39: Find the synergies

Write your to-do list for this week – errands, work projects, family responsibilities, hobbies and so on. How about synergizing some of this stuff to include connection? You could:

- Walk the dog with a friend to the post office and back.

- Attend the yoga class with your buddies and factor in time to chat. Make an evening of it.

- Invite friends over for a fence-painting or flower-planting party where you chat as you work and have them invite you and your crew over to return the favour.

- Host a slow-cooker or meal-cooking party for a few friends where you each bring ingredients for a meal for 12 and each make that meal while you natter. Bring plenty of Tupperware/boxes with lids and utensils then divide your own meal into a few portions for each of them and take home portions of their meals to freeze. (This saves money as well as time.)

STEP 40: Ritualize and routine your diary dates

One of the "top five regrets of the dying", from palliative care nurse Bronnie Ware's book of the same name, is not having stayed in touch with friends. Put effort into ensuring golden friendships do not slip by.

Routines take less thought or action to plan as you've already planned them. Knowing that the last Saturday morning in every month is brunch date, for example, you'll know not to double-book and will have more regular get-togethers. Book annual or quarterly spa breaks with old friends; monthly or seasonal "explore" dates where you become a tourist of your local area with friends/family; and weekly, fortnightly or monthly phone or video calls with family members and/or friends. It's too easy to sit and watch TV together, but interaction generates laughter and positivity resonance, which strengthens bonds. Teamwork and team play, especially of the family kind, boost positive emotions and strengthen relationships.

STEP 41: Bridge community connections

We may be better connected virtually than ever before but, in reality, studies have revealed that many still feel alone. As well as forging strong bonds with those we're fond of, it's important to build "bridging connections" in the real world to unite different groups within a community.

Think of ways you could bring people from different backgrounds together through a shared interest, to build what Harvard professor Robert Putnam calls the "social capital" of a community. For example, you could plant a community vegetable garden; fill an old phone box with books to create a street library; or make a street directory of useful and entertaining stuff available to be borrowed from you and your neighbours.

STEP 42: Accept differences and focus on what you admire

Consider your team (this might include your partner, siblings, friends). The best and most effective teams have skills and characteristics that complement each other – where one person's strengths make up for another's weaknesses. While you may have a good deal in common, try to celebrate and appreciate your differences too. One person's aloofness may come in handy as a calming influence when the other is in a panic, while another person's attention to detail or need for control might be annoying, yet useful in certain circumstances.

Jot down positive traits that you value in each other. Relationship expert Dr John Gottman found that happier couples exchange at least five times as many positive statements as negative ones. So, practise focusing attention on what's right with people, rather than what's wrong. Praise effort and encourage rather than criticize.

....

....

....

....

....

STEP 43: Develop deeper compassion

Think of a relationship where you are experiencing difficulties and a misunderstanding the other person may have about you. What would you tell them to help them better understand what they have misunderstood? If you gave them the same opportunity what might they say? Is it worth writing to each other in a compassionate way to share/investigate further?

Now, imagine that person as a child (if you have a photo of them as a child, even better). Remind yourself we're all just muddling through and we all make mistakes. It's easier to judge and criticize than it is to praise and empathize. Yet the latter is far more rewarding and has a wide-ranging social impact. For example, researchers have found that teaching empathy in schools reduces bullying. For self-compassion, find a photograph of yourself as a child and keep it on your phone for when you're giving yourself a hard time.

Chapter Eight
M IS FOR MEANING

The meaning of life is meaning: whatever it is, wherever it comes from, a unified purpose is what gives meaning to life.

Mihaly Csikszentmihalyi

The values you hold dear, the things you care about and the contribution you give to the world – these fundamental essences of who you are spell out your purpose, your "why", and give your life meaning. The level of meaning in life contributes to how much we flourish.

Meaning decreases depression and anxiety, according to the University of Colorado's 2008 Meaning in Life Questionnaire, while a 2012 college student study found that those with a strong sense of purpose had higher levels of self-esteem and felt more satisfied with their lives. But what is meaning and how is it different to purpose? Meaning is subjective. It's a sense that our life has inherent value and significance. That life fits into a larger context and makes sense, based on what we do and experience, and how we contribute and respond to life.

Purpose, defined by purpose coach Carin Rockind, is "the driving force behind who you are and the active way you uniquely impact the world". Purpose and meaning are intertwined because purpose is a prerequisite for giving our lives hope and meaning.

Why meaning matters

Meaning matters to our well-being for several reasons, not least because, as German philosopher Friedrich Nietzsche famously said, "[S]He who has a why to live for, can bear almost any how." It's far easier to cope with our present and have hope for our future if we have a focal why; a reason for doing what we do that provides meaning. So says a well-being and personal growth study of 338 university students in 1996, which revealed that optimism is easier to cultivate, and obstacles easier to rise above, when we are committed to a set of values, a cause or a meaningful purpose.

In his book, *Man's Search for Meaning*, Austrian psychologist and Nazi concentration camp survivor Viktor Frankl relays how he found that those not sent to the gas chambers yet still forced to endure harsh camp conditions were more likely to survive if they had a purpose to live for. This is partly because purposeful actions and responses generate hope – and hope creates meaning. As Robert Kennedy once said, "Each time someone stands up for an ideal or acts to improve the lot of others… he sends forth a tiny ripple of hope." Essentially, purpose acts as a kind of "hope fuel". Yet our purpose need not be world changing, nor must we go on a quest to find our calling, which can lead to purpose anxiety. Rather, living a meaningful life with purpose can simply involve a series of authentic actions where you follow your spark, let your values guide you and use your strengths to contribute in some small way.

STEP 44: Turn purpose into a verb

Purpose coach Carin Rockind says we can struggle with the expectation of finding a purpose when we view the word as a noun, such as "teacher", "mother", "writer" – as something we want to be or have. Conversely, when we see purpose as a verb – a "doing" word – it can feel more achievable: for instance, to inspire, teach, build, support, heal, create, care for, appreciate, love. By turning purpose from a noun into a verb, we can find opportunities to be purposeful *right now*, rather than seeing purpose as something to strive for.

If our purpose was to become a teacher/writer/entertainer, we can seek out opportunities to teach, write and entertain *right now*, by using the qualities and skills we already have. For instance, you could teach work colleagues something that will help them; write and pass on advice to those who might need it; or find ways to entertain people each day. This makes it easier to enjoy the journey and find greater balance. For when our sense of purpose is central to our daily actions, we can find harmony between what we want to achieve and who we already are.

Finish the following sentence. My purpose is to be… (e.g. loving, grateful, kind, creative, inspirational, entertaining):

....

....

Consider some small actions that will enable you to be more "that". Write them here (e.g. to create, I will devote 10 minutes each morning to writing/ sketching):

To ...., I will ....

....

....

....

....

....

Meaningful response to adversity

When someone we love dies, we may not particularly care about learning from that loss or creating meaning from it – we just want that person back. Yet – as much as we would swap lessons or meaning for a single additional moment with that person – the lessons (and love) are what we are left with. And love never dies. In the absence of having the person there with us, doing something purposeful that offers hope to others can help give death some meaning and provide some comfort. This realization that something good can come from something so devastatingly bad is why people start or fundraise for charities in honour of a dearly departed family member. Such purposeful action generates joy from pain, hope from despair; it turns something tough into something tender, makes something heart-warming from something heart-breaking.

Doing something, taking control, being active rather than passive, creates hope and meaning, whether that's appreciating nature more because they did, raising money for charity, starting your own charity, or simply sharing your story. It's one of the reasons why I write books to help people make the most of life, because losing my parents at a young age amplified how precious life is. Moreover, the actions we take after adversity can cultivate a kind of co-destiny with someone who has died, so they can live on and leave a combined legacy with us. Making a difference, no matter how big or small, makes meaning.

STEP 45: Find meaning in adversity

There are, according to Viktor Frankl, two types of meaning:

1. Ultimate meaning: purposeful direction we are headed toward, defined by what matters most to us/our values, which can serve as a kind of compass, rather than by an achievable goal. For example: serving, inspiring or teaching others; contributing in some way.

2. Meaning of the moment: the choices, responses and decisions that we make in each moment.

We can gain meaning from what we give, what we receive and how we respond. In 1964 Frankl framed these three core values into a "meaning triangle", to illustrate how anyone can cultivate meaning in their lives.

1. Creativity: how we contribute to the world via self-expression, be that through our work, art, good deeds, inventions, writing, music, volunteering, charitable efforts and so on.

2. Experience: what we receive from the world via our experiences to create "meaning of the moment" from our interactions, relationships, connections with nature, culture, spirituality and so on.

3. Attitude: how we respond to and interpret situations, circumstances and other life-conditions via our own perspective and considering alternative perspectives.

What adversities have you faced in your life?

....

....

....

What actions could you take to make meaning from them? To honour a person or experience? To help others? Brainstorm ideas here.

....

....

....

STEP 46: Capture meaningful moments

Reflect on what is meaningful to you. Give yourself a project over the course of a week by taking photographs of anything that holds meaning for you. Seek out sources of meaning, including childhood memories and mementos, serene spaces that you love to visit, loved ones or books that have positively impacted your life, and take photos of those meaningful things. At the end of the week reflect on the photos. Consider why each item is meaningful for you and write in your journal about this experience. This exercise was the basis of a study carried out in 2013 where student participants felt a greater sense of meaning and life satisfaction, and more positive emotions, as a result.

STEP 47: Do what you love and love what you do

Living purposefully is partly about fanning the flames of what fascinates and inspires you – whatever sparks your curiosity. "What are you fascinated by?" is a far lighter question than, "What is your purpose in life?"

What lights you up? When are you in your element and most at ease with what you're doing? Consider those activities for which simply participating provides its own reward. Write them down and commit to doing more of them.

....

....

....

Why do you love participating in these activities so much? What is it about them that you enjoy? E.g. the feeling of accomplishment from writing or the pride from watching someone master what you've taught them? You need not become a teacher or writer to experience these feelings – you can teach or write anyway.

....

....

....

....

What inspires you? What do you want to master? What do you want to become better at? If you didn't need to earn money, what topics would you pay someone to learn more about?

....

....

....

What are you curious about? Any problems you are keen to solve? This could become the way you earn your living, or it could be something you do to add a splash of meaning to your life.

....

....

....

STEP 48: Find your forte and use it

Deploy your character strengths. Revisit your VIA character strengths results (see page 27) and schedule into your planner ways to use your signature strengths. Positive psychologists believe you can boost your life satisfaction if you identify and then use your signature strengths as often as possible. For example, if creativity is a strength, redesign a room, journal, create a scrapbook or photo collage, or paint some birthday cards. If kindness is one of your strengths, schedule in some acts of kindness. Jot down ideas for strength-utilizing activities here:

....

....

....

Write an acrostic poem using the first letters of your name (or simply words that describe your strengths and qualities). I'll go first:

Caring   Resilient
Hopeful   Yay-sayer
Enthusiastic   Loving

Your turn:

....

....

....

....

....

STEP 49: Uncover your values

Which values are most important to you? What do you/would you teach your children? What values do you want your life to reflect? In the list below, circle all that appeal most to you, then prioritize five to ten that are your absolutely non-negotiable values in life.

Adventure	Integrity
Cleanliness	Justice
Community	Kindness
Compassion	Love
Cooperation	Loyalty
Courage	Peace
Creativity	Play
Discipline	Positivity
Diversity	Reliability
Effort	Resilience
Encouragement	Respect
Environmentalism	Service
Equality	Stability
Excellence	Strength
Family	Success
Friendship	Teamwork
Generosity	Timeliness
Gratitude	Tolerance
Growth	Tradition
Honesty	Unity
Humility	Wisdom
Individuality	Wonder

How do you wish to be remembered? What would you want your tombstone epitaph to say?

....

....

....

Does your life currently reflect these values? Do you need to set any boundaries to realign with them? Based on your values, what could you say yes/no to this week/month/year?

....

....

....

CONTRIBUTION

The purpose of life is not to be happy. It is to be useful, to be honourable, to be compassionate, to have it make some difference that you have lived and lived well.

Ralph Waldo Emerson

How you contribute to the world gives your life meaning, so how you use your strengths, values and experiences to make an impact can elevate hope (for yourself and others) and add more meaning to your life.

STEP 50: Consider your contribution motivation

Which causes do you care most about? What breaks your heart and/or makes you cross? If you had a magic wand, what would you change in society? List the causes you care enough about that you'd be willing to contribute time or money in service of them.

....

....

....

Who do you feel most drawn to speak on behalf of? This may be global or local. Your family or local community? Your generation, gender or ethnic group? The environment or wildlife?

....

....

....

What kind of world do you want to live in?

....

....

....

What would your TED talk be about? Imagine you have a chance to share a message with the world that goes viral – something that matters deeply to you, that you are knowledgeable about and that could positively impact people's lives. What do you want the world to know?

....

....

....

How being of service also serves us

Kindness is meaningful. Whatever we spend on being kind – be it time, money, energy or effort – we also receive back, via boosted positive emotions, a greater sense of meaning and improved social connection. This is what the Buddhist monk Matthieu Ricard calls "psychological economics". In terms of well-being, both giver and recipient win.

People who volunteer have higher levels of happiness, less depression and anxiety and a greater sense of purpose. Evidently, being supportive is as good for us as being supported. In fact, altruism is the number-one positive intervention to boost well-being. According to Martin Seligman and Ed Diener in their 2002 *Psychological Science* research paper on very happy people, performing acts of kindness boosts our well-being more than any other intervention tested.

According to Howard Friedman and Leslie Martin's *The Longevity Project*, a book which assesses the results of a study that began in 1921 to explore who lives the longest and why, the clearest benefit from social relationships came from helping others, with those who supported and cared for other people living to a ripe old age.

The best way to cheer yourself up is to try to cheer somebody else up.

Mark Twain

But why is helping other people so helpful to our own well-being?

- Givers' glow. Kindness activates our "nucleus accumbens" – the reward centre in our brain. In a study by the University of Oregon in the USA, the pleasure/reward centres in people's brains lit up and released endorphins (hormones that reduce pain, induce happiness and relax us) during voluntary charitable giving, providing evidence of the "warm glow" that we feel. This explains why performing – or even thinking about performing – acts of kindness produces a tangible "helpers' high".

- Sense of belonging. Through generosity without expectation, altruism can help us root ourselves in our community. We are more likely to become a valued member of our community when we are kind to those within it. Furthermore, kindness fosters togetherness and cooperation.

- Good feelings last beyond the good deed itself. Dopamine levels increase not only when we give, but before and after our acts of kindness – during the planning stage and the "afterglow". According to the National Academy of Sciences, brain scans reveal that planning a donation activates the mesolimbic pathway, which is associated with feelings of happiness and increased levels of dopamine. Long after volunteering, many people feel an improved sense of self-worth, less stress and a lasting period of increased well-being.

How and what to give

Winston Churchill was right when he said, "We make a living by what we get. We make a life by what we give." But how can we incorporate giving into our daily lives and what can we give?

How to give:

- Perform multiple kind acts in one day. Studies have shown that "chunking" kindness (carrying out five acts of kindness on one specific day per week, for a period of ten weeks) has a greater impact on our happiness than sprinkling kindness (performing one act of kindness each day for ten weeks).

- Mix it up. Choose a variety of kind acts rather than repeating the same ones. Acts of kindness that connect you with recipients directly, so you can see the impact of your giving, tend to have the greatest effect on the giver's well-being.

- Pay it forward. Harness the contagion of altruism to create a ripple of kindness by suggesting that your recipients "pay it forward". Do a good deed for three people and ask them to forward it to three more people.

What to give:

- Physical, practical donations: gifts, flowers and charitable donations of money, clothing and food.

- Your time, presence and expertise. Help a neighbour out, or volunteer. One of the reasons why the Danes are thought to be one of the happiest nations is that almost half of them volunteer, with 70 per cent being active recently.

- Shared experience. Prosocial spending – where you buy concert tickets or pay for meals or spa days – has the added bonus of connection with those who join you in the experience.

- Random acts of kindness. Sellotape coins to vending machines, bake cakes for neighbours, or be a flower ninja (I've had fun buying £1 bunches of daffodils and dropping them at friends' doorsteps or giving to mums on the school run).

STEP 51: Choose how and what to give

Write a giving list. Choose some from the ideas listed above and jot down your own additional ideas for giving below:

....

....

....

I knew my forty-third birthday was going to be a difficult one for me as I would turn the same age my mum was when she died, so I wanted to do something to honour her kind-heartedness. A kindness marathon felt like the perfect idea, so I set a budget and made a plan. My daughter and I baked biscuits and distributed them to neighbours, including those I'd never met. I paid for the orders of three people behind me in the queue at Starbucks, gave flowers to strangers at bus stops and delivered baked goods to friends and nurses. I slipped encouraging messages into library books and stuck coins and "free parking" notes to parking meters. One woman was so overcome that she opened up to me about her recent divorce followed by the loss of her brother – and I listened. We connected over a simple £1 offering. Altruism works as it opens the door to connection, delivers positivity for giver and receiver and makes life meaningful.

Both the planning and the "afterglow" boosted my well-being and during the day itself I felt more connected to humanity than I'd felt before. Although I was completely wiped out at the end of the day, I awoke feeling replenished, connected and joyful, and that feeling lasted longer than I'd expected.

RESPONSE

As Viktor Frankl's two types of meaning suggest (see page 107), a meaningful life is also about how we create meaning from the choices we make and the responses we give to every moment – even the difficult experiences we inevitably face.

STEP 52: Find the meaning in your life experiences

What might be a different way of looking at challenges that you've faced or setbacks you've endured?

....

....

....

....

How might you use that fresh perspective to shape your future?

....

....

....

....

How might you use the meaning you've uncovered to help others?

....

....

....

....

Chapter Nine

A IS FOR ACCOMPLISHMENT

You are never too old to set another goal or to dream a new dream.

Les Brown

Improving areas of life that enhance our life satisfaction enables flourishing – be that via achieving better work–life balance, developing stronger friendships and loving relationships, or improving material comfort and safety. Or by gaining freedom from pain and disease by improving physical health; career accomplishment to improve financial security or greater satisfaction at work; or education to develop knowledge, self-mastery and mental health. Even though awareness of the hedonic treadmill and arrival fallacy reminds us to focus on enjoying the journey and cherishing experiences, accomplishment still matters to flourishing.

There are three stages to accomplishment:

1. Understanding *why* you want to accomplish what you do.

2. Knowing *what* you want to accomplish.

3. Figuring out *how* best to achieve it.

These are the three stages we'll work on in this chapter.

Why accomplishment boosts well-being

Accomplishment isn't just about providing us with whatever we hoped for. As we know, the happy feelings we gain from getting what we want don't last long before we return to our "set-point" due to hedonic adaptation. However, accomplishment earns its place as a branch of well-being because of the other benefits it provides.

- Accomplishment boosts our self-esteem and our self-efficacy because goal achievement reveals what our strengths are, which boosts our self-belief and builds our faith in our capabilities.

- The process of celebrating, rewarding and savouring our wins helps us to become our own cheerleaders – an important role to take on.

- Striving to accomplish goals taps into that all-important hope that we know correlates with well-being.
- Accomplishment offers opportunity for growth, which is at the core of flourishing.

STEP 53: Balance growth with gratitude, accomplishment with appreciation

Focusing so intently on the end goal that we forget to cherish our current contentment can dilute the reward of accomplishment. The "I'll be happy when..." fallacy simply postpones happiness in lieu of achievement; especially given how quickly the novelty wears off, once we've grown accustomed to whatever we've achieved. To flourish then, gratitude and growth must go hand-in-hand. Such balance is vital as it enables us to enjoy the journey toward our destination. Plus, as renowned professor and author Deepak Chopra says, "Intention is much more powerful when it comes from a place of contentment than if it arises from a sense of lack or need."

If we can maintain a good balance between gratitude for what we already have/all we've already accomplished with imagining how grateful we'd feel once we've accomplished all we hope to have, gratitude can make the journey more enjoyable and the growth more likely. Hope, goal-setting and gratitude are a powerful combination. So be sure to make your gratitude practices at least as frequent as your goal-setting ones to remind yourself what you already have to be grateful for. Balance is key!

STEP 54: Free yourself to imagine possibilities

Take a deep slow breath in... and exhale. Imagine that once you have finished reading this book and set it aside on a table or bookshelf, something magical happens – all your worries and concerns, all the problems you've been wrangling with, have vanished. And, even better, everything will go well from now on, whatever you choose to do. Have a think – now there is nothing more to worry about or struggle with, what would you do differently tomorrow? What would you focus your attention on and spend more time doing? Who would you spend your time with? What would you say yes to and what would you say no to? Where would you go? How might you speak to others differently? How might you speak to yourself differently?

By shifting your attention away from what you *don't* want (i.e. problems, worries and what's lacking) to what you *do* want (solutions, hopes and what's possible) and away from any self-doubt toward a mind free of worry, you can look through a lens of hope, and see opportunities and possibilities with greater clarity. You'll picture more precisely what it is that you want from this one precious life of yours and your dream accomplishments will appear more vibrant.

Take a deep breath in for a count of three and breathe out for a count of five. Let us begin.

STEP 55: Define your dreams

Imagine your fairy godmother appears and grants you a wish to create your dream self, living your dream life. First, you must describe to her what your best-possible self is like, listing your qualities, quirks and whatever makes you uniquely you when you are at your most content and radiant.

My best possible self. This is me when I am:

....

....

....

My best day. Imagine you are living your dream. How do you spend your morning, afternoon and evening, and with whom? Where are you and how does it feel? Get specific. Write non-stop for a few minutes about what you see, feel, hear, touch and smell.

....

....

....

....

....

....

My dream life. If money was no object, you had all the time in the world and success was guaranteed, what would you do with your days? Define your dream life, where all is well with your relationships, career and health. What does having and experiencing all you've ever wanted look like? Also consider what would you rather try and fail at then never try and do, even if failure was likely? This shifts the focus away from the destination of success toward the journey of enjoyment.

....

....

....

....

....

University of Missouri students who undertook that "best-possible self" exercise, and then wrote about their dream life for 20 minutes for four days, were happier and more optimistic three weeks later, while undergraduates who visualized positive future experiences once a week for eight weeks reported increased well-being six months later.

When your inspiration flails, stop, put down whatever you're doing, walk barefoot on the grass, breathe deeply and ask yourself that question: *what do I truly want?* Then journal about it for a few minutes and take one small action toward bringing that to fruition. You might be surprised by what happens next. Some other exercises to help tune in to what matters most:

- Revisit page 33 to see what makes you feel envious or inspired. Remember, when you see a lifestyle, job role, relationship, someone's style that you either envy or admire, these feelings are giving you clues about what you want.

- Write a letter to your future self. You can upload your letters to futureme.org and set them to be sent to you at some point in the future. It'll be a wonderful surprise to receive a note from past you in one, three or five years' time. Write about something you are currently wrangling with and your hopes for the future.

- Write a letter *from* your future self. Visualize walking through a door to meet them. Your future self is happy to see you and has a reassuring presence. They tell you all is well: you did and have what you wanted and became who you wanted to be. Notice what your future self looks and smells like. Take in your surroundings – where are you living? What are you wearing? Who are you with? Now write a note to your present self from this future self. What do they want to tell you?

STEP 56: Turn your dreams into goals

The next step is to turn all of those future hopes and dreams into actionable and achievable goals.

- Write them as if you've already accomplished these goals. For example, if your goal is to buy your dream home by the end of the year, instead of writing "This will be the year that I buy my own home", write: "I now own and live in my dream home" followed by the location and date by which you aim to achieve this.

- Frame goals using positive terminology. This makes them "approach goals" rather than "avoidance goals". For example, turn "Stop eating junk food" into "Eat healthy food, including seven portions of fruit or vegetables each day". Goals should be framed in the positive because, according to author and coach Caroline Adams Miller, approaching a goal in this way uses less mental energy than avoiding it.

STEP 57: Define *why* you wish to accomplish this

Now explain why these goals matter to you; why do you want what you want? There is always more to your desires than you think. For example, top athletes often aren't competing just to win; there will be other reasons, such as making their family proud, overcoming adversity and fulfilling a long-held dream. So, if you list as a goal, "A dream home of my own in the next village", ask yourself what would having that home in that location give you. Your "why" behind your dream home might be safety, security, comfort, status, confidence, belonging, pride. Your "why" behind your dream to write a book might be to empower and inspire people, to leave a legacy, to make your family proud, to set a good example for your children. Find your motivation. Source your inspiration.

Goal ....

My why ....

Goal ....

My why ....

Goal ....

My why ....

Now consider other ways to bring about those whys right now. For instance, if your dream home "why" is to give you feelings of warmth and belonging, consider joining a local community group, moving your furniture around to feel more homely, or distributing candles and cushions to feel cosier. That way, you can enjoy the journey and experience similar feelings that attainment of your goal would provide now, rather than waiting until you get there. This will also make visualization exercises (see page 126) easier because you'll already be aligned with the feeling that accomplishment will give you. Now you've got clarity on *what* you hope to accomplish and why, it's time to figure out how.

How to accomplish your goals

You are far more likely to achieve your goals if you write them down as you plant the seed of your dreams. When you take action toward accomplishing them you water those seeds. But first:

- Make goals specific and realistic. They should be sufficiently challenging to make them worthwhile, but realistic enough to successfully achieve.

- Set "primers" to support your goal. "Primers" are cues or reminders paired with your goal that act as stimuli to shift behaviour. For example, an "eat veg" sticky note on the fridge; workout gear on a bedside chair; meditation bells next to the morning coffee; encouraging screensavers. Our unconscious reaction to external cues directs most of our activity, so words, scents and sights can make us more likely to take specific actions. Studies have shown performance enhanced after viewing an image of a runner winning a race and students more likely to clean up crumbs when sitting next to a lemon-scented cleaning product.

- Prevent pitfalls with implementation intentions. These are statements outlining what you'll do should a pitfall arise. This method can triple the likelihood of goal achievement and uses less energy (and willpower). For example, "If I feel hungry after 9 p.m., I'll have a piece of fruit and one square of chocolate."

- Share goals and report progress. Having someone to hold us accountable can make us far more likely to achieve our goals. Because if nobody knows we're avoiding action toward our goals, it's easier not to bother. Accountability reduces our excuses and reminds us that other people care.

- Plan your rewards. Gardeners don't wait until every flower is in full bloom to enjoy their green space. They delight in each new bud and cherish the time they spend tending to each blossom. Similarly, we shouldn't wait until we've achieved our goals to enjoy our lives. Delight instead in each small step you take and celebrate immediately. Planning rewards you'll give yourself when you accomplish goals is motivational and helps you enjoy the fruits of your labour not only once in full bloom, but also while they (and you) grow.

- See failure as feedback and go again. There's no such thing as failure, unless we fail to learn from our mistakes, which can always be rectified by trying again. If we don't achieve what we set out to, we learn. And in learning we grow. From Edison to Dyson, successful people attribute their success to the valuable lessons they learned from mistakes they made along the way.

- Write a self-contract to seal your commitment. According to a behaviour modification study by Caroline Adams Miller, participants who wrote a contract for themselves were 86 per cent more likely to meet their goal, and students who drew up a contract to complete all assignments did more work than students who didn't. Let's do that now.

STEP 58: Write a self-contract

My specific goal is to: ....

....

.... by ....

Action steps include: ....

....

I will use the following primers: ....

....

I will reward the completion of each action step with: ....

....

I will share my goals with: ....

....

I want to achieve this goal because: ....

....

This is my commitment contract to myself.

Signed .... Dated ....

Here are more ways to accomplish your goals:

- Affirm goals in the present tense. Every time we repeat our affirmed goals, the neural pathways around that thought strengthen into a belief and activate your subconscious mind (and the Universe) into bringing opportunities, people and resources to you to help you reach them.

- Affirm goals to create and manifest self-fulfilling prophecies. Stating something as already true can help bring it to fruition. This has worked for me. In 2003 I wrote down, "I am a published author, I have met Anita Roddick." My *Small Business Start-Up Workbook* was published two years later, with a foreword written by Dame Anita Roddick after I not only met her but worked for her too. Here are my affirmations:

> *Thank you for our continued good health.*
> *We've moved into our very own dream home.*
> *My book is a bestseller.*
> *All is well in our world.*

Your turn. My affirmations:

....

....

....

....

🔹 Visualize achieving your goal. Visualization uses the power of our imagination to show our brain what is possible – and, rather magically, to the brain our achievement seems real. Visualization takes place in the cerebral cortex – the same area where our thinking, language and problem-solving happens. The brain can't tell the difference between what it thinks and what it sees, so it reacts to *visualized* images as though they are real. When we imagine something we fear, our heart rate quickens as if we were facing that fear for real; the same is true when we visualize something we want.

Scientifically, visualization works because it:

🔹 Activates the placebo effect, because we become more confident in the possibility of our goal, which primes us for action.

🔹 Activates the attention bias, by deepening awareness around thoughts that support our belief about achieving the goal.

🔹 Induces positive emotions more than verbally discussing the goal does.

STEP 59: Visualize living your dream life

If your goal is to write a book, picture yourself walking into your local bookshop and seeing your book on the shelf; pick it up and feel the cover; sniff it, flick through the pages. See it in your mind's eye: your name on the cover, the design and colour, the title. Experience the emotions you would feel – the pride, the gratitude, the delight. To maximize the power of visualization, picture the result of your achievements (outcome visualization) and how you got there (process visualization).

🔹 Picture the process as you watch yourself working toward the goal. For example, imagine yourself writing your book manuscript and receiving an email with a publisher's offer. See yourself phoning a friend to share the news and them saying, "I knew you could do it!"

- Picture the outcome you desire, visualize what living your dream life looks like. Read through your written summaries of your dream day, best self and life first, then create your future in your mind's eye as if it is already your present. See yourself there. Write non-stop for a few minutes about what you see, feel, hear and smell. Explore your environment: what colours catch your eye? What sounds? Breathe in your surroundings. Now focus on what you're doing: Who is there with you? Why are you smiling? Picture yourself telling someone how proud you feel about achieving this goal. And, believe in your vision. Allowing doubt to creep in can be like cancelling a cosmic shopping list order mid-transit. Have hope and trust.

- Make a vision board as a primer. Cut images and words from a magazine that illustrate your vision. Pin it in a place you look at frequently.

MOVING FORWARD WITH INTENTIONAL ACTION

Dreams remain in your head, or on the page, until you take action. Those seeds need watering to flourish. And it's far easier to stay passionate about where you are headed if you know *how* you are going to get there. Working toward goals is good for us. Our neural circuitry likes intentional action as it helps us gain clarity over uncertainty. Making decisions and setting intentions positively engages the pre-frontal cortex, calms the limbic system and overcomes activity of the striatum, which influences movement and balance. The combination of these factors pulls us away from negative impulses and reduces anxiety.

With action we become the author of our own story, with a storyboard plotted out, rather than aimlessly ambling through life. While we may sometimes miss targets or find that life delivers unexpected plot twists, if we approach our goals as steps in the right direction and use failures as learning opportunities (mistakes are stepping stones too) our goals will feed our growth. When we voluntarily decide to take action that results in an accomplishment, our brains get a boost of dopamine. We feel better when our decisions – rather than chance or obligation – lead to good things happening. That's why goals and ambitions must come from you and be aligned with what you truly want, rather than from those pesky "shackles of should" or external expectations.

STEP 60: Plot each action step toward your goal

To get you from where you are now to where you aim to be, break down the pathway to each goal into small stepping stones, outlining what action you will take and when, with clear deadlines. Breaking up goals in this way motivates the unconscious mind to accomplish them, as the emotional part of the brain prefers small, easy actions that provide immediate feedback. Write your goal and the stepping stones to get you there beneath the example below.

Goal – Have more energy and live a healthier lifestyle by the summer.

Stepping stone 1 – Drink a glass of water every day when I wake up, before lunch and before my evening meal.

Stepping stone 2 – Take the stairs instead of the lift each day at work.

Stepping stone 3 – Cycle to work twice a week.

Stepping stone 4 – Go for an evening swim/dance class once a week.

Stepping stone 5 – Go to bed 30 minutes earlier without my phone (read instead).

If you engage in consistent action and take a step toward your goal every single day – you WILL reach your destination. Plot these actions into your flourish planner on pages 148–9.

Chapter Ten
V IS FOR VITALITY

Energy is eternal delight.

William Blake

A study published in *Frontiers in Physiology* in 2018 discovered that children have higher energy levels than well-trained athletes. I remember that feeling of vitality as a child, leaping barefoot across the lawn, climbing trees, roller-skating, cartwheeling, riding my bike everywhere. As children we move effortlessly from one activity to the next, full of energy, enthusiasm and vitality. I even won the merit cup at school for sport enthusiasm (I remember being a little embarrassed that I won it for enthusiasm rather than prowess), but back then I had vitality in abundance.

However, over time, for many of us life has become far more sedentary with much of the physicality removed by labour-saving gadgets, vehicles in which we sit and technologies that mean we can do so much more from the comfort of sitting.

Moving more is also motivated by the rather scary suggestion by author Nilofer Merchant that "sitting is the new smoking", because we now sit for an average of 10 hours per day. Sitting has a negative impact not just on our vitality, but our physical and mental health. Our bodies are meant to move – they were designed for motion. Back when we were hunter-gatherers we'd walk, climb and run constantly. The more vitality we have, the better we function.

What is vitality?

Vitality essentially puts the "being-well" into "well-being" as optimum wellness is about what Flourishing Center founder Emiliya Zhivotovskaya defines as "building a flourishing mind housed in a flourishing body". To function optimally, both mentally and physically, we need energy. Vitality is the state of being strong, alert and energized. So, given the well-documented mind–body connection, vitality is vital to flourishing.

We know that self-care is health-care, and not just the kind that involves pampering sessions and time spent cosied up with a favourite book (as important as that kind of self-care is). When we choose to look after our bodies, we pay a deposit into our personal vitality bank and gain an energy boost. Conversely, when we don't, we make a withdrawal from our energy reserves and can feel depleted and low on energy, which makes everything feel more arduous. Running on empty – as a result of a lack of sleep, exercise and/or nutrients – can be bad for us. We can only truly flourish when sufficiently nourished.

Restorative activities, such as a good night's sleep, a physical workout and well-balanced diet, replenish our energy reserves and boost our vitality, so we can cope better with life's inevitable challenges. To optimize our vitality, experts suggest that we move more and sleep, eat and breathe well. This helps balance the polarities of calm and stress, and keeps our energy banks in credit.

STEP 61: Check your subjective vitality levels

To establish our vitality levels, i.e. how full of energy we feel, first check in with this Subjective Vitality Scale (Ryan & Frederick, 1997). Rate the following statements based on whether they are very true or not at all true:

NOT AT ALL TRUE  VERY TRUE

1. I feel alive and vital.

2. Sometimes I feel so alive I just want to burst.

3. I have energy and spirit.

4. I look forward to each new day.

5. I nearly always feel alert and awake.

6. I feel energized.

This will determine how "vital" you feel. However, this is a subjective scale, rather than a measurement of how energized your body and mind are. Thanks to their innate intelligence, as an ecosystem they will respond to actions we take. Five ways to improve vitality are to:

1. Move more.

2. Sleep well.

3. Eat well.

4. Breathe well.

5. Connect with nature.

So, let's explore ways to introduce more of these aspects into your life.

Move more

We've long known the importance of exercise on health. Hippocrates called exercise and nutrition "medicine" in the fourth century BCE, while Greek ideals of exercise led to the Olympic Games and the tai chi exercise system first emphasized graceful movement as a route to health and vitality in 200 BCE.

Exercise energizes but, more than that, as mind–body medicine reveals, movement has the power to lift mood, boost brain power, relieve exhaustion and reduce depression. That's all thanks to the feel-good endorphins released when we exercise, which help us think clearer and feel better. Physical activity reduces anxiety and stress levels, lowers rates of mortality and disease and increases muscle strength. It improves bone and heart health and reduces cholesterol and blood-sugar levels. As well as boosting our quality of life, regular exercise also helps improve our quality of sleep by quietening our pre-bedtime mind-chatter. Hooray for moving our bodies then! According to the UK Department of Health: "Physical activity is effective in the treatment of clinical depression and can be as successful as psychotherapy or medication, particularly in the longer term."

The recommendations for good physical fitness are activities that elevate the heart rate for 20–30 minutes, three to five times per week, with children recommended to be active for an hour each day. However, even 1 hour per week lessens health risks for adults too. The suggested 10,000 steps a day was set by a pedometer company that, with the Tokyo Olympics coming up, were keen to sell more products. They came up with this arbitrary (and often unachievable) number. The truth is, while upping up our step count is good, getting out and active for just 20 minutes per day offers a 30 per cent reduced risk of depression and an almost guaranteed way to lift mood compared with not moving, which can make you feel worse. In fact, if we generally feel fine and have no health conditions, not exercising for just one week can make us feel sluggish.

So, why can it be such a struggle to fit exercise into our daily lives? Perhaps it's because of the way we view it – as a chore?

STEP 62: Find the fun in daily movement to enjoy exercising

What if we made exercise so fun it became something to enjoy rather than endure? The next time you need motivation to get your body moving, try the following:

- Revisit the list of the activities you used to love doing as a child on page 88, from climbing trees and roller-skating to making up dance routines in the garden. Could you participate in any of those now? Find out if roller discos still operate in your area. Or why not combine a trip to a dry ski slope with a quick go on the ringos, pop to your local ice rink or give rock climbing a go?

- Have a kitchen disco either routinely with your own playlists or spontaneously boogieing to the radio. While dancing energetically gets your heart rate up, researchers from Northumbria University also found classical music, such as Vivaldi's Spring concerto, enhanced alertness and memory and enabled participants to respond quicker and more accurately to test tasks than those who completed tests in silence. So prancing round the kitchen to classical music will boost your post-disco productivity too!

- Join your children, younger siblings, nieces or nephews in some fun in motion. Play hopscotch, go geo-caching or explore your local area on a family bike ride. Play football/soccer using "jumpers for goalposts" or have a trampolining championship.

- Hold a headstand competition. Doing headstands not only improves brain function; if done regularly, MRI studies reveal that headstands can improve mood and release stress.

- Try new activities. From body combat, to aerial yoga or BungeeFit.

- Practise ancient movement techniques. Investigate Ayurveda – the ancient Indian philosophy of health – which led to yoga, first codified in 600 BCE.

STEP 63: Use exercise as a means of transport

The Dutch and the Danes view cycling as a means of transport rather than exercise. In Copenhagen there are five times as many bikes as cars, with Danes cycling an average of 1.5 km (1 mile) every day. Given the good-mood endorphins released during exercise, this may partly explain why Danes top the world's happiest ratings so often. List the journeys you must take often and consider ways you could use your legs to get you from A to B more frequently, via walking, cycling, running, roller-skating or scootering.

STEP 64: Use your body's natural biological rhythms to schedule movement, work and rest routines

Biological rhythms are regulated by an internal clock in our hypothalamus to control sleep and alertness, body temperature and so on. Circadian rhythms play out over 24 hours, such as our sleep–wake cycle. Ultradian rhythms play out over shorter increments. Our basic rest–activity cycle (BRAC) plays out in 80- to 120-minute cycles. During sleep we tend to have 90 minutes of non-REM rest and 20 minutes of REM sleep in 110-minute cycles. During wakefulness it's helpful to our vitality (and productivity) to continue this rhythm with 90 minutes of activity then 20 minutes of rest, rather than ignore our body's need for breaks.

- Use your body's own natural BRAC to determine when it's best to exercise (at the bottom of your BRAC) or rest. The average person is most alert and energized late morning and mid-evening, and at their lowest ebb mid-afternoon and first thing. A workout or kitchen disco first thing and a brisk mid-afternoon walk or power-nap would boost energy levels.

- Schedule regular "stretch and hydrate" 20-minute breaks at 90-minute intervals to give your body the mini-recovery period it craves. We tend to experience an energy lull after an "ultradian sprint" of 90 minutes of working, as signalled by yawns, hunger or a restless lack of concentration (cue checking of social media and procrastination – far better to set an alarm to remind you to stretch, run up and down the stairs, take a walk and drink water rather than ignore the signs and stay sitting).

- Schedule moving meetings and/or set up a treadmill workstation where you can walk and talk (or type) simultaneously during the "activity" cycle. Walking meetings are often more productive than others because walking cultivates creative thinking. According to a Stanford University study, we are between 60 and 80 per cent more creative when we walk, compared with when we sit still. And this effect can last long after we've returned to a sitting position. Walking is a bone-strengthening, mood-lifting, ailment-avoiding wonder of a physical activity and puts less pressure on knees than running.

- Make movement routines habitual. The more you can automate specific physical activities and make them routine, the more movement will become habitual. Habit-making has the added bonus of saving energy by conserving willpower and removing the mental effort involved in decision-making. For example, if you arrange to cycle to work with a friend on specific days, you're no longer faced with the decision of whether to drag yourself out of bed to exercise on those mornings – the decision is already made.

- Schedule regular periods of cardio and strength-training exercise into your week. Experts recommend three periods of cardiovascular activity and one period of strength training per week, or a minimum of three exercise periods where you break into a sweat.

SLEEP WELL

Sufficient sleep is essential to flourishing. Sleep boosts our vitality as our alertness and energy increase and our concentration, creativity, memory and performance are improved.

Yet, contrary to popular belief, sleep isn't just about switching off. In fact, what many don't realize is that sleep is as restorative as it is restful. While our brains, heart rate and breathing may slow while we slumber, our brains are not inactive while we sleep. Over the course of the night, we drift through consistent cycles of light sleep, deep sleep and dreaming. We seal our memories during light-sleep cycles and our bodies produce growth hormones during deep sleep to stimulate tissue growth and muscle repair and support immune functioning.

Meanwhile, according to neuroscience, dreams facilitate both learning and memory. During our REM (rapid eye movement) dream cycle, which we tend to drift into every 90 minutes, our brains race and our heart rate rises while our subconscious minds work through our worries and declutter our concerns. So, dreaming restores our mind and deep sleep restores our body.

Lack of sleep can impact the memory-storing hippocampus part of our brain and cause us to feel clogged up, as we didn't get the chance to declutter our minds or restore ourselves. No wonder feeling tired can negatively impact mood and performance. What's more, we are – according to a British Psychological Society *Research Digest* study – more sensitive to fear and anger when we're tired. We ideally need between 7 and 8 hours of sleep per night, with teens needing between 8 and 10 hours and children needing around 10 hours, depending on their age.

STEP 65: Establish good sleep hygiene

Good sleep hygiene involves healthy sleep rituals, getting to know your own tiredness cues and creating the best conditions for a good night's sleep. Try the following:

- Create a sacred and serene sleep space. Make sure it is dark, quiet, uncluttered and cool enough, with sufficient fresh air. Have a supportive pillow, house plants for good air quality, and only use lamps that provide a warm glow to encourage the release of sleep hormone, melatonin.

- Avoid caffeinated drinks and foods that cause heartburn after lunch as caffeine can block the sleep-promoting hormone adenosine. Try foods containing natural sources of melatonin, such as tart cherries, goji berries, milk and pistachio nuts.

- Unwind in good time before bed. At the start of that wind-down period stop using your phone or other electronic devices. They give off blue light that suppresses the production of melatonin and can keep you awake.

- Replace screen time with other activities. Read or journal. Empty your mind of tasks by writing your to-do list. Soak in an Epsom salt bath, play a guided meditation, try restorative yoga or Yoga Nidra.

- Go to bed and wake up at the same time each night and morning. Have consistent routines for eating, exercising and sleeping at similar times.

- Use progressive muscle relaxation to help you drift off. Tense and release each muscle group in your body, from your toes to your head, as you slowly inhale and exhale.

- Count blessings rather than sheep. Picture all that you are grateful for in visual form so you drift off in a positive mood rather than ruminating.

- Take an afternoon nap for 10–20 minutes, maximum, but only if you don't suffer from insomnia and if it doesn't impact your main sleep. According to one study, brief naps where you do not slip into REM sleep can make you more focused, creative and productive and can soak up sleep debt from less successful sleeps.

EAT WELL

We all know nutrition, or the lack of it, can impact our physical health, but what we eat can impact our mental well-being too. Eating well boosts our physical energy, our mental mood and enhances sleep. But healthy eating isn't about restriction, it's about eating well-balanced, nourishing food that fills us up with the right nutrients. Again, routine can help as decisions about what to eat take up a lot of brain space. According to research by Cornell University, we make an estimated 226 daily decisions about food.

STEP 66: Make food choice easier

Try these ideas:

- Plan your meals and snacks each week so you know ahead of time what you are eating and when. Aim for two to three portions of calcium-containing foods, at least five portions of fruit and vegetables (but aim for seven), along with nutritious protein sources, wholegrains, balanced snacks and small portions of carbohydrates at each meal. Carbohydrates are energy giving, but are easy to overeat, whereas protein helps keep us fuller for longer.

- Choose food from a position of self-care rather than self-control. Focus on what you can eat rather than what you can't, and on what you'll gain rather than what you'll lose. Rather than having a goal of losing weight, focus on what you'll gain from establishing good eating habits – better health, a healthier lifestyle and more energy.

- Teach yourself moderation rather than prevention. By focusing on choosing nourishing foods, rather than on limiting "bad" foods, you can create a healthier relationship with what you put into your body. Restriction and depriving ourselves of certain foods can lead us to want them more or eat more of them "post-diet". Far better to see changes in food choice as a long-term shift in a healthier lifestyle.

- Choose good-mood foods. Blueberries, almonds, spinach, tuna, oranges, bananas, sweet potatoes, brown rice, avocado, Brazil nuts, sardines, oats, lentils, chicken, turkey, yoghurt, dark chocolate and oysters have all been shown to enhance mood.

- Drink more water. Our brains function so much better when our bodies are well hydrated. Use an app or an alarm to remind you to drink water every hour, or use cues. For example, drink water every time you send an email or finish talking on the phone. Since investing in a big 2-litre bottle of water with times of day listed down the side, I've had much more energy.

Eat more fruit, veg, nuts, seeds and fibre to decrease inflammation. Aim for seven servings of fruit and veg and 30 g of fibre each day. Try antioxidant-rich berries and green smoothies for a wonderful way to consume more fruit and vegetables, especially leafy greens. Add spinach to all smoothies as it is relatively tasteless, but oh-so good for you. Junk food affects your mood and too much sugar can induce depression. Prebiotics can moderate this, as can foods that nourish a healthy microbiota for good gut health as that stimulates mood. Grains, greens and other veggies should take priority along with seeds, nuts, herbs, oils and ferments. Aim to eat fish, poultry and eggs two to five times per week and reduce red meat and sweets.

BREATHE WELL

Sometimes the most important thing in a whole day is the rest we take between two deep breaths.

Etty Hillesum

Our breath is a direct link to our own nervous system. Inhaling activates our sympathetic nervous system, while exhaling activates our parasympathetic nervous system. This means our breath can give us greater control over how we respond to external stimuli, but there is also great duality in breath mastery. By this I mean we can use our breath to give us more vitality or serenity; to help us feel more alert or calmer; to rejuvenate or relax us. Exhaling for a longer count than your inhale can calm you, while inhaling deeply then pulsating an exhale as if blowing out a candle multiple times can increase oxygen and improve alertness. Just one minute of conscious breathwork can clear the body of stress hormone cortisol and leave us more alert and at ease, while deep abdominal breathing can help diffuse difficult emotions such as fear, anxiety and anger, and even release trauma.

The problem is, most of us don't breathe how we were designed to. At least, not any more. When we are born, and as children, we use our whole lung capacity to breathe. It's no coincidence that we're at our most energetic when we are young. As we age, the stressors of everyday life cause our body to naturally brace and tense as an automatic protection response. But our busy stressful culture has caused us to brace more often than is necessary. This bracing makes us breathe shallower and quicker, breathing from our chest rather than our belly.

Consequently, researchers have found most of us don't use our diaphragms as our primary breathing muscle (as designed) to breathe in and out. Rather, many of us breathe "up and down" in our neck and shoulders, bracing our diaphragm rather than using it properly by inhaling using our belly, which should go outward as we take in air, opening up our lungs.

Widely, we are not taking a full breath, so are not engaging our "rest and digest" mode much. Moreover, this kind of shallower breathing can cause our vagus nerve to message a stress signal to the brain to remain in fight-or-flight mode. This can affect our vitality, including our sleep and digestion, our nervous system, how we relate to others and how we respond to stress. So, learning to breathe well (horizontally, rather than vertically) is important for our vitality. (Horizontal breathing is also known as belly-breathing or diaphragmatic breathing, and draws oxygen into the bottom of the lungs.)

Awareness is always a good first step, so noticing ourselves bracing means we can learn to do this less often. We can also remind ourselves regularly throughout the day to breathe using more of our lung capacity. With practice, we can breathe how we were designed to (how we do as children) and, thanks to muscle memory, our body can remember and is more likely to continue breathing in that way.

STEP 67: Practise breath mastery

We tend to be so mind-oriented that breathwork (like yoga) can help us become more body-oriented and soothe our nervous system. There are different types of breathwork to try. Here are two:

Practise belly-breathing (diaphragmatic or "horizontal" breathing)

Belly-breathing increases the supply of oxygen and nutrients to the body, boosting energy and vitality, stabilizing blood pressure, slowing heartbeat and expanding attention span. It also improves core muscle strength. To engage our diaphragm, when we inhale, the aim is to expand the tummy outward and narrow it on the exhale.

- Try belly-breathing first by lying on your front and breathing deeply into your belly as it expands on the inhale. You'll be more aware of your tummy expanding this way.

- Next, lie on your back. Place one hand on your belly and the other on your chest. Feel your belly rising as you inhale deeply through your nose, to the count of six. The hand on your belly will rise while the other hand remains still. Exhale through your nose to the count of seven. The hand on your belly will fall back. Repeat five times. When you breathe in, let the air fill your belly, then breathe in again filling your chest. When you exhale, your belly button should get closer and closer to your spine. This exercise enables you to deepen your breath, strengthen your lung muscles and stimulate the vagus nerve, which runs from the brain to the abdomen and aids relaxation and rejuvenation.

Practise double breathing to oxygenate your cells

This signature practice of the "Living Yoga Method", created by yogi Steve Harrison of the Yoga Sanctuary, can help reset and recalibrate the mind and body to enable optimal functioning. It serves to detoxify, oxygenate, energize and rejuvenate.

- Take two deep breaths (a double breath) in through your nose as you push your belly out, exhale a double breath out through your mouth and pull your belly in. Do this five to ten times.

- Next, take a double breath in through your nose, using the first breath to fill your belly and the second part to lift the breath up into the chest. Exhale a double breath out through the mouth. Do this five to ten times.

- Finally, take a double breath in through your nose, lifting the breath straight up and into your chest. Exhale a double breath out through your mouth. Do this five to ten times. These three stages of breathing exercise the lower, middle and upper lobes of the lungs, strengthening the respiratory system.
Now, take a slow, deep single breath in through your nose, hold the breath in for

2 seconds, exhale out through your mouth until you have just a little air left in your lungs. Now you will find you don't need to breathe at all. Hold your breath out for as long as you comfortably can and go "within" into "dynamic stillness". This is about you taking control and staying calm without breathing.

- When you feel the need to breathe again, take a recovery breath and hold the breath in for a count of 12 to consolidate the overall effects of the practice.

- Exhale out through the mouth and relax into the tranquillity that follows the practice.

As breathwork couch Rebecca Dennis of Breathing Tree says, "Breathwork is the most sustainable medicine we have on the planet." But to maximize its effectiveness, it's important to use it properly. Here's how:

Practise conscious connected breathing at regular intervals daily

Inhale into the belly, then into the chest and exhale out through your mouth. Repeat continuously, so it feels like a rolling wave. This three-part breathing method is the foundation of conscious connected breathwork. Take ten or a hundred breaths in this way and you'll feel the flow of energy and open yourself up to greater vitality and less mental noise.

- Breathe in through your nostrils. Doing so provides you with the opportunity to clean and warm the air you breathe in before it reaches your lungs. As such, it is better for your health than mouth breathing.

- Focus attention on your breath whenever you feel anxious. This is the core of mindfulness, where, whenever you are distracted, you bring your attention back to your breath repeatedly. A calming practice, mindfulness can be expanded further by noting what you can see, hear, taste, touch and smell in the moment.

Use breath to re-engage rational thinking

When anxious, our rational brains can become temporarily unavailable as our fight-or-flight response hands control to our emotional brain (our amygdala). During this irrational state, we may react impulsively and can become panicked when worry spirals build and our rational brain remains out of action. The only way to regain control and become calm is to breathe deeper and slower, but when life feels stressful, it can be difficult to get mindful. This is why experts recommend practising mindful breathing when we are calm; it helps the body learn how to self-regulate, so the next time we're feeling overwhelmed, we can pause and breathe more consciously.

When we anchor our attention to the breath, our nervous system steps down a gear from its high-alert status and stops pumping adrenalin and cortisol. This slower state calms us down. Practise it now and write down how taking deeper, slower breaths made you feel.

....

STEP 68: Practise slow breathing

Practising slow breathing has been found to reduce depression and PTSD as it brings the balance back from an overactive fight-or-flight stress response to the soothing rest-and-digest parasympathetic nervous system. The lung capacity of Mount Everest climbers was four times greater for slow-breathing participants in one study. The control group, who breathed twice as fast, needed oxygen to complete the climb. What's more, slow breathing also improves our heart rate variability, positively impacting the heart's capacity to adapt to stress.

People can breathe between four and 24 breaths per minute, with the average around 12. How many breaths per minute do you breathe when breathing naturally? Time yourself and write down your results:

....

Try slowing down your breathing to five or six breaths per minute. This will help you to optimize control of your breathing muscles and help you restore balance to your nervous system and vitality.

Releasing trauma

Breathwork can also help us release tension and trauma if done with the help of professional facilitators. When our diaphragm is unlocked and we are guided through a conscious or transformative breathing session, our breath can greatly influence our mental, emotional and physical state.

The floodgates can open, as anyone who has experienced a facilitated breathwork session will tell you. When I attended a breathwork session with breath facilitator Rebecca Dennis, I released trauma I didn't even realize I'd been holding on to. The experience was incredibly emotional, yet comforting. There are various types of breathwork, from conscious connected breathing to transformational breathwork, but I recommend practising with a trained practitioner.

CONNECT WITH NATURE

Just as there is duality in breath mastery, so too is there a duality in what nature can give us. Like breath mastery, connecting with nature can relax and invigorate us, soothe and stimulate us, calm us down and lift us up.

Nature, like gratitude, is a wellness wonder drug and it's available for free to anyone, anywhere. All you need to do is look up or look out and tune in to your senses to reap the benefits. Being outdoors has a profound impact on how much we flourish. Like plants, we need sunshine, water and fresh air to thrive. Natural light stimulates our hypothalamus activity, and the amount of serotonin and melatonin we release, all of which affects our sleep, mood and appetite.

Research shows we are friendlier and exhibit more prosocial behaviour when the sun is shining and the sky is blue, and also when we are awestruck by the magnificence of trees, whatever the weather. One study showed those who looked up at very tall trees for just 1 minute experienced awe and then demonstrated more helpful behaviour than those who looked up at tall buildings for the same amount of time.

Indeed, researchers like to compare green versus urban, walks through parks versus shopping centres and, in doing so, have discovered the powerfully nurturing effect of nature on our well-being. In a *Journal of Environmental Psychology* study, half the participants were led at the same pace on a

15-minute walk on a tree-lined path along a river, while the other half were led on a 15-minute underground walk through tunnels. Those walking in nature had significantly higher vitality-change scores where they felt more energetic, vital and alert. So woodland and parkland walks invigorate and energize us more than walking in urban environments for the same length of time and at the same pace. Seaside strolls along the coast breathing in all that sea air also help us feel and sleep better.

The power of green and blue

From our evolutionary biology that remembers trees as provision of shelter to the sensory appeal of the colour green, I explore the power of trees for boosting our well-being in my book, *Tree Glee: How and Why Trees Make Us Feel Better*.

Both green and blue spaces are calming. Trees act as natural stress-relievers. Breathing in their essential oils (phytoncides) can reduce our blood pressure, calm us down, boost anti-cancer protein production and enhance our immune system capability. Even looking out of a window at a view of trees can quicken healing and reduce inflammation. We have a similar psychological response to water too. Oceans, lakes, rivers and waterfalls bring on a meditative "blue mind" state, a term coined by Dr Wallace Nichols, plus a variety of other well-being effects.

Scientific evidence from a study by the Center for Environment, Health and Field Sciences in Japan's Chiba University has shown that forest bathing (the practice of consciously taking in and immersion in the forest atmosphere, through a sensory experience of the sights, sounds and smells of the forest) reduces blood pressure, heart rate and cortisol production, while boosting the immune system and levels of well-being. Hence why the Japanese made the practice of *shinrin-yoku*, or "forest bathing", part of a national public-health programme in 1982. It is now a national pastime. So, whether you opt for a woodland walk, wild swim or seaside stroll, to amble alongside a meandering river or climb a hill or mountain, let nature nurture you by committing to getting outdoors more.

STEP 69: Get out into green and blue space

We know about the need for "white space" in terms of resting sufficiently, but we need to give ourselves some green and blue space too. Here's how:

- Visit the seaside. Twice-weekly coastal visits have been shown by environmental psychologists to boost mental health, while beach strolls (like woodland walks) have been shown to help people sleep longer than those walking in urban environments.

- Forest bathe. Walk slowly through the woods soaking up all you can see, hear, smell, taste and touch. To learn more, my book *Tree Glee* explores how and why trees make us feel better.

- Go wild swimming. Cold-water immersion is an effective way to treat depression, according to a 2018 *British Medical Journal* study. Research safe outdoor swimming spots online.

- Exercise outdoors. Practice tai chi or yoga in your local park or in your back garden. Cycle through local scenery. A University of Canberra, Australia, study discovered that outdoor activity can help reduce anxiety.

- Grow and tend to plants. The bacteria found in soil, "mycobacterium vaccae", activates the brain to produce serotonin, a neurotransmitter associated with feelings of happiness, calm and focus, and is responsible for regulating mood, social behaviour and sleep.

- Go bird watching. A recent bio-science report showed a positive link between the number of birds, trees and shrubs people see and their mental health, especially during the afternoon, when there are more birds to watch.

STEP 70: Create a vitality plan

Commit to taking a tiny step (or a series of them) to improve your vitality. Perhaps you could do 10 minutes of outdoor yoga and breathwork every morning? Or commit to drinking a green smoothie three times a week? You could eat a piece of fruit on the school run or to and from work? Or go to bed 10 minutes earlier? Try one small step for 21 days, and then another step. Each is a significant step toward better self-care. It takes 21 days of repetition to create new and replace old habits, for neural pathways to shift. Before you know it, your 10-minute walk has become a 30-minute stroll or a 20-minute run; your daily smoothie habit has led you to eat more nutritious breakfasts; your breath mastery has enabled you to focus your emotional energy on what matters most to you.

Write down: What could you do to make a 1 per cent increase to your vitality?

Movement: ....

Nutrition: ....

Sleep: ....

Breathwork: ....

Nature connection: ....

FLOURISH PLANNER

This is the final piece of the flourishing puzzle, so now it's time to schedule actions into your own flourish planner, so you can commit to doing more of what calms you down, lifts you up and enables you to flourish. First, refer back to Step 8 where you defined what good enough looked like for you.

While using your flourish planner, remember to use three different colour pens to schedule – one for work, one for rest or self-care and one for play.

	MONDAY	TUESDAY	WEDNESDAY
6AM			
7AM			
8AM			
9AM			
10AM			
11AM			
MIDDAY			
1PM			
2PM			
3PM			
4PM			
5PM			
6PM			
7PM			
8PM			
9PM			
10PM			
11PM			

THURSDAY	FRIDAY	SATURDAY	SUNDAY

Schedule chunks of time off each week/month/season, then schedule in:

Daily

- Moments of stillness (white space)
- Gratitude walks in nature (green space and blue space)
- Exercise (set routine)
- Stretch and hydrate breaks
- Conscious breathing practice
- Vitality plan activities
- Flourish list activities (between one and ten per day)
- Singing
- Reading time
- Goal stepping-stone actions

Weekly or fortnightly

- Self-care activities
- Meal plan nutritious meals for the week ahead
- Outdoor activities (gardening, walking, etc.)
- Thoughts to court time
- Journaling time
- Art therapy time
- Talking therapy time (with a professional or a friend)
- Watch the sunset and/or sunrise
- Schedule an awe movie/a laughter movie
- Mini awe-adventure
- Reminisce time
- Gratitude journal/jar/photos, visit, walk
- Engaging activities pick 'n' mix

- Relationship-nourishing list activities and synergized activities
- Practise a loving-kindness meditation
- Message friends
- Kitchen disco
- Geo-caching and other fun activities
- Yoga session
- Synergized coffee/class/walk with friend

Monthly or seasonally

- Update mood playlists
- Arts and culture day (gallery, museum, opera, theatre)
- Decoupage or pottery painting session with friends
- Watercolour/creative workshop
- Paint cards for friends
- Music making session/lesson
- Live music gig
- Sound bath
- Forest bath
- Flowful activities (see STEP 30 on page 86)
- Meaningful activities (see STEP 51 on page 115)
- Playtime
- Visit friends who live further afield
- Spa breaks/brunch/explore dates with friends
- Spa day solo
- Community activities
- Giving-plan activities
- Set and share goals
- Visualize

CONCLUSION

Your life can always take a different path and direction. Wherever you've come from and wherever you are now, you can flourish by purposefully scheduling tried-and-tested strategies into your days, and by feeling *all* that you feel, rather than avoiding difficult emotions. You can find balance between the positive and the negative, reframe inaccurate, unhelpful thoughts into more accurate and helpful ones and build on what's good.

I hope, through the steps and exercises in this workbook, you've found ways to soften into finding more acceptance, balance and compassion so you can have hope, see yourself and your world in a better light and bring the balance back; to accept what you cannot change and change what you can.

And I hope with this development of deeper awareness, you can choose curiosity over judgement more often, so you can live your life through a more loving lens. Because this is it – our one and only time on Earth – a life in which we can flourish or languish depending on what we think, what we feel and what we do. And that, my friend, is up to you.

ACKNOWLEDGEMENTS

It's been 10 years since I wrote my first book on the topic of flourishing, and the friendship and love I've received has enabled me to flourish. Supportive relationships are so integral to our well-being. So, thank you to my soul sisters (you know who you are), and to all friends who see, hear and encourage each other. Thank you all.

I thank and honour my late parents, Denise and Roger, who were the most loving and supportive parents anyone could wish for. Thank you for laying the foundations from which I could flourish. I dedicate this book to you both.

Huge thanks and love also to my amazing daughter, Brooke (who always knows the right thing to say to make people feel better), and to my other half, James, for all your support, kindness and patience over the years. I love you both.

Thanks to Emiliya Zhivotovskaya of The Flourishing Centre in New York for all the wonderful Change Agent training work you do. I will be forever grateful for your tuition in the field of Positive Psychology.

And thank you to the wonderful team at Summersdale. I'm so glad you were able to see with me the kind of book this was always meant to be. It's always a pleasure to work with you and I'm so grateful for the effort you each put into the books you so lovingly create with your authors.

ABOUT THE AUTHOR

Cheryl Rickman is a *Sunday Times* bestselling author and ghostwriter of 26 self-help, mental health and business books; a positive psychology practitioner and a Wellbeing Ambassador for the Network of Wellbeing.

After her parents' lives were cut short, Cheryl decided to devote her life to helping others to make the most of their own precious lives, through the books she writes and the workshops she gives. She specializes in writing empowering, practical books to help people fret less and flourish more.

Her most recent books include *Tree Glee*, *Navigating Loneliness*, and *The Happiness Bible*. Having qualified with a Certificate in Applied Positive Psychology in 2016, Cheryl also speaks about The ABC of Flourishing™ and the power of trees in making us feel better, at festivals and retreats across the country.

Cheryl lives with her partner, daughter and two Labradors in a country cottage in Hampshire, UK. She is a lover of nature, has an overflowing bookshelf and her favourite colour is rainbow.

You can find out more at **www.CherylRickman.co.uk**

NOTES

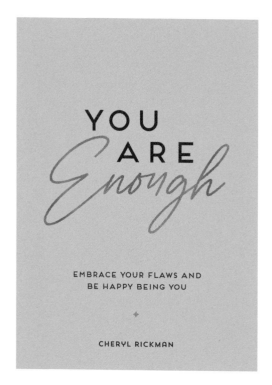

YOU ARE ENOUGH

Cheryl Rickman

Paperback

ISBN: 978-1-80007-002-8

- Have you ever experienced imposter syndrome?
- Do you often find yourself seeking approval from others?
- Is beating yourself up getting you down?

Then this book can help you.

With thought-provoking advice, a step-by-step action plan and a simple method to challenge your inner critic, *You Are Enough* will help you embrace your flaws and celebrate your unique awesomeness. Let go of the myth of perfection, finally stop comparing yourself to others, and learn how to be happy with all that you are.

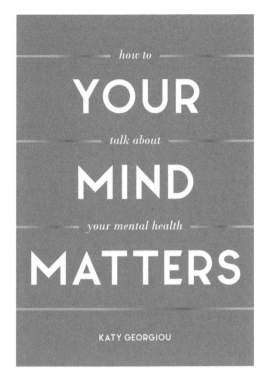

YOUR MIND MATTERS

Katy Georgiou

Paperback

ISBN: 978-1-80007-410-1

Build your confidence and open up the conversation

Talking about your mental health is one of the most important steps you can take towards better well-being, but for many this can seem daunting. For anyone struggling to initiate the conversation, this book is here to end the stigma around mental health and help you communicate how you're feeling.

Topics covered include:

- Anxiety, stress and depression
- Suicidal thoughts
- Mindfulness and self-care
- Opening up about your mental health
- Seeking further support

Have you enjoyed this book?
If so, why not write a review on your favourite website?

If you're interested in finding out more about our books,
find us on Facebook at Summersdale Publishers, on Twitter at
@Summersdale and on Instagram at @summersdalebooks
and get in touch. We'd love to hear from you!

Thanks very much for buying this Summersdale book.

www.summersdale.com

For a list of references, please visit www.CherylRickman.co.uk